Dance of Duality

Ishaan Nag

INDIA · SINGAPORE · MALAYSIA

ISBN 979-8-89233-587-4

In Memory of my Grandpa, Sujit Kumar Nag.

Keep inspiring...

Foreword

This is highly philosophical, most of it goes above my head, however it urges me to read further as it sounds mysterious. It makes me curious what lies ahead. "Dance of Duality" written by Ishaan Nag, a 16 year old boy talks about our deepest inner fears, the courage to face our confusions and our mixed emotions related to taking decisions.

I congratulate Ishaan for being fiercely brave to be able to deal with this duality.

This may be his third book but I am sure there are many more to come in the near future.

God Bless,

Seema Sapru
Principal
The Heritage School
Kolkata, India

Acknowledgement

I have written this collection of poems after I joined the International Baccalaureate of The Heritage School, Kolkata. This program has helped me to retrospect on my own strengths and limitations. It has instilled, and is still instilling in me the ability to explore how and why we do what we do, why I feel what I feel. It has given me the ability to be more empathetic, and have the ability to shift perspectives to that of other stakeholders. I thank the school for helping me be a better learner and lend me more depth of character, which has directly helped me to write this poem, predominantly based on perspectives, how others would feel. It would be amiss to not acknowledge the immense effect my teachers have caused on my ability to retrospect and be a critical thinker. I would like to thank our *Principal Seema Ma'am* for being accessible to her students when in need of assistance and for being so candid in her advice to her students, of whom I am proudly a part of. I would like to thank our *Headmaster Daryll Sir* for being so supportive of every endeavor and initiative his pupils undertake. When I used to be a part of his History classes, I was infected by the immense passion and love he had for the subject, and that inspired me to adopt the same passion at whatever I do. I would like to express my gratitude to our *IBDP co-ordinator Kavita Ma'am* and *Trina Ma'am,* my homeroom teacher *Anindita Ma'am,* along with my subject teachers *Shaoli Ma'am, Piyali Ma'am, Alokananda Ma'am,*

Aparna Ma'am, Prajna Ma'am, Rimashree Ma'am, Chinmoyee Ma'am and Jaya Ma'am, for they have been readily available and accessible to help me whenever I required guidance. Lastly but definitely not the least, I would like to thank my parents for the guidance and certainty they have provided me with my work, myself and my life. Not a single word of this collection would have been possible without all of you.

Special Thanks

I would like to extend my gratitude towards the great work done by my friends **Niharica Sengupta, Kashvi Dhanani** and **Adrijaa Pal** in making the sketches accompanying some of the poems. They have truly succeeded in capturing the essence of each poem assigned with the sketches, and I have only to thank their experience and passion for that. They have worked tirelessly and with dedication, and I can only reiterate for them.

Niharica has been honing her skills in visual arts ever since she embarked on her journey to explore her mettle in art, which dates back to the very start of her education, from her pre-primary years. Initially a means of developing a skill merely for scholastic purposes, art had taken her by storm and developed into a passion. Impressionist, abstract, realist or just plain art for beauty's sake, regardless of inner meaning, she has a broad base of expertise.

Roald Dahl's Matilda fused with a blunt, artsy soul-that's **Kashvi**. You can often find her creating art, devouring books and humming Taylor Swift songs. An art fanatic since the age of 10, she has been wielding paintbrushes, sculpting and crafting artworks. When Rogerson said,"for all the girls who found themselves in books" she definitely meant Kashvi.

An experienced artist and an art aficionado ever since she could read write and paint, that's **Adrijaa**. Starting as an intrinsic liking to the aesthetics so natural to the world of painting, she now uses art to express her inner emotions and ideas she wants to convey to the world. She doesn't restrict herself to a specific art form, yet just like everyone has their favourites, Adrijaa draws special inspiration from the human anatomy, taking great pleasure in the designs they inspire and inculcating them in her art. As Henri Matisse said, "Don't wait for inspiration. It comes while working", and Adrijaa's art evolution exemplifies just that.

Contents

Didn't we, at some point of time in our life, rejoice the fact that we are not embroiled in a situation we had rather not be in, though caused by us? We have observed, be it parents, colleagues, friends, closed ones, or mere passerby, a small comment turns to deadly riots, a small slap turns to a mob lynch, a small action or inaction turns to a cold war. This poem aims to rejoice these guilty, strange facts of life and humanity.

A Stray Ember

When she thought he threw the garbage out, but he says he forgot,
Brushed aside by a smile from the innocent culprit, yet the tension is taut.
"Oh yes, it's just garbage, it will surely not smell when it starts to rot",
"It will invade the house, not the vaporizer, the decadent I want".

And thus a stray ember, the mere presence of a filled plastic bag,
Has started a war, has broken ties we thought were cemented, a war which will drag,
Until it digs all, yet aggravates each problem, like the world's worst shovel,
I only yearn to not be noticed for once and made the unwilling judge, for heavy is the gable.

And the heart during the uneasy ceasefire, where glances are mutually hidden,
Even silent conversations shunned upon, the conscience disease-ridden.
The garbage is forgotten, the report cards, the detentions barely remembered,
An inferno is sparked, the flames standing by forgotten, all for a stray ember.

What a pity the judge who hopes to not be, is
criminal himself.
What a relief, they forgot who was really supposed to help,
Dispose the garbage, pack the luggage nice and tight, and
throw it away,
What a relief, the stray ember, the wars, the shouts, the hurt,
saved me, as furtive glances I display.

Of course, emotions are subjective, but this poem takes us on a ride to explore our seemingly irrelevant emotion of feeling guilt at ditching the old and established. It tries to discover the aimless, blank emotions we often have, the willingness to submit to the wishes of the universe we often don't recognize. One could say, no matter how pompous it sounds, this poem is a memoir to track such an aimless journey.

Where It Takes Me

I wonder where the keys I hover around will take me today.
I wonder how the antiquated ink with its quilted tip would say.
Would it's nip break like a petulant child's attempt at
non-cooperation?
Would it lead my fingers to spell out long lists of taunts,
forgetting cessation?

Maybe it would sputter out a last spray of the blue used-to-
be ecstasy,
Like a last breath, a last mirthless smile, at this new-found,
blasphemous apostasy.
It has turned away from my cushiony criticisms, it can
hear no more,
It refuses to realize it's fault, for it refused the "lesser ones" to
afford it, and also write lores.

It refused the chance to create legends, for it didn't fancy
their rags,
Its feather refused to be more than a decorative nuisance,
while the nip drags,
The hand adorned with jewels, and only that hand,
The fractured hand, the sickly hand but a brimming mind is
dismissed, like a hairy strand.

I wonder when it will be reborn, as a prized, vintage possession.
I wonder how many pages it had wasted, on the hands of a struggling writer with frustration.
I wonder, if, in its last ballet in my hands, it is grudging or hates me,
I wonder now, how will it take to its "alien, alternative", but for now, I wonder where it takes me.

Past, present and future: all of them are vastly different, be it for the better or worse. Perspectives change, ideas change, morality changes, definitions change. And in this change, you shall be surprised, and witness others being surprised, at different timelines from theirs. This aptly named poem is thus truly an anecdotes of surprise.

Anecdotes of Surprise

I have seen a peasant talk with his head held high, and be able to read and even write!
I have seen an innocent woman treated as such, her dignity and aspirations respected,
Instead of deeming her a witch, I have also seen,
Someone who didn't make merry and mingle in a tavern adorned by the sickly sweet of rotten yeast.

I have seen a lower, heathen man of another creed who behaved the same as we did,
Felt the same way we did, smiled and helped the same way we did, yet died more deaths than us,
Heard scorns more than us, pelted with stone instead of respect like us.
I have heard of a king of the colonized race who possessed more than we could ever loot and hunt.

I have heard of neighbours, who visit each other on weekends,
Who know each other's faces, who smile at each other not as an involuntary obligation,
But in delight of seeing a friend. I have seen them open their curtains, and wave at each other.
I have seen someone on the metro close the escapist abode of blue light and shallow advertisements to gaze out the window.

I have seen a passerby help up a fallen comrade,
I have seen them offer a visible helping hand, instead of an apathetic, avoiding gaze.
I have seen a person, too satiated to eat,
Let the scrawny beggar eat his leftovers, when he begged for it.

I have seen a person, who really used his legs,
I have seen a person not even grunting, to
maneuver her hand,
Around the packet of chips, to pick one and savour,
This dexterity fascinated me in a world of life-like statues.

I have seen a person, who really used his fingers to write a word or two,
I have seen a few people who didn't forget the names of the people who gave birth to them.
I have seen a mere person write, and even talk with a fellow being,
I have seen a person refuse more food when satiated and full.

You can't really blame our subject of mock in this poem. The wish to blame is an innate human wish. It's like thirst and hunger. It is really a truly terrible feeling to feel hatred and self-pity, but no one to possibly blame. It's painful, and that pain is immortal. The thing of sorrow however, is how less we restrain ourselves, how much we are blinded by this crushing thirst and hunger. I do not need to provide examples of when the blame game goes inhumane; human history is enough.

Chew Toy

Do you miss your chew toy, my snarling, growling little darling?
Do you miss the helpless squeak it makes when you are furious,
On a minor inconvenience not even caused by this innocent little ball.
Do you miss the shriek it makes? Do you miss the pierce your teeth make?

My dear little thirsty mutt, do you miss the sadistic pleasure,
When the spit from your mouth falls on an undeserving thing, acid pricking it,
The acid in you which that little piece of rag didn't throw on you, or give a reason to possess.
Do you feel the submitting, distressed feeling in your empty, hungry mouth?

My dear little lover of cuddles, do you lack the vent,
Do you lack the victim whom you can freely beat and bruise and squeeze and tear,
And render useless, colourless, hapless, worthless, lifeless?
I know you do; I know your pain, I shall strive to provide you with another toy,
A goat this time, maybe, a scapegoat, to replace another innocent chew toy.

Continuing the theme of changing perspectives, this poem highlights the differing values different people attach to different things. This poem aims to highlight the value people assign to different things.

Bargaining Price

From a show-piece, a souvenir, to a loved one's sweet, salty wet memory.
From an unnoticed substance on the vast surface of earth, to an object of reverence, prayer.
Some shall scoff at even the prospect of paying, while some shall sell their souls,
For the same, irrelevant yet holy drop of water, the particles of dust, with no price and priceless at the same time.

A subjective price, a poetic price (but is this art we are talking about?)
What price is right? When does this stop? When does a negotiation go south?
While any sane person would bargain enough to draw the ire of the seller,
Sometimes such cold sanity is what propels astronauts to leave probably, and maybe the bargain is undeserved.

A great bargainer is praise and a spit of acid depending on the worth.
A rug is worth peanuts, a prayer mat worth a soul.
A frame is worth as scrap metal, though a picture makes it a chalice of youth.
A piece of metal is worthless, but with buttons and a screen?
Invincible, priceless.

It is next to impossible to even attempt to tell what purpose, what lessons this teaches us. But do our musings always need to have a use, a purpose? Can't we celebrate the very aimlessness of our eyes and mind, the unreal situations we are either in or carve ourselves?

Dream House

I was introduced to the word aeons ago, but I only now
really know what 'surreal' means.
I now know how surreal feels, how it looks. I no longer
use it aimlessly, as means of pretending to be part of the
Zeitgeist.
Welcome to this dream house of cozy breakfast nooks,
Where the warmth of waffles wafts in the air, and seduces
like a siren.

Welcome to this dream house, where a hostel seems inviting,
Where bunker cells and tiny prison beds are dainty.
Close your eyes, and you will conjure something in reality,
Open them, and they fade, like your limits and
expanding horizons.

A dream house where it is so hot one can't help but shiver,
Where the sweet fragrance of even the usual shampoo
reminds you of sweet ambiguity,
Reminds you to look sharp for those pleasantly ambiguous,
sophisticated public shrouded in mystery,
That surely intellectual, highly cultured world, but not sure
which kind.

And I am not curious enough to find out, but enticed
enough to follow,
Be the paparazzi who is willingly welcomed, and dignified,
and be a part of a club.
Though not a fiery integration, one that burns the cloak,
Of mystery, of exotic perceptions, but I would take part
surely, nevertheless.

Welcome to such a dream house, where blankets cause
sweat, and their absence: cold.
Welcome, where words of confirmation and surety only
increase signs of indecisiveness.
Where every event is an ironic paradox, every expression
an oxymoron,
Yet in this dream house, one revels in this simple, easy
complexity, where straying away from a topic is taunted, yet
the tone does allow.

Inspired by a dark, stormy day and an irresistibly terrific earthy smell (which gets one addicted as soon as one gets a sniff of it), this poem is here to pay homage to the destructive power of nature and thunderstorms, and the rain which both floods and fertilizes the world and cleans off her filth.

Thunderstorm

I pray the thunder occupies your chest, its thump tramples your heart,
Or more precisely, the parasite inside, and cleanses all the dark inside,
Let the rushing, rambling rain be ready to clean out the gutters of your conscience,
Let the burning lightning integrate with your soul, and be you.

I pray that the storm takes away your guilt, and bring back your lost innocence,
And bring back the kites, the paper boats that tide had snatched away from me, so long ago.
I pray the earthy smell makes me love the cloudy dark,
I pray it clears my hoarse throat and let me chant the terribly terrific epic of apocalypse.

I pray this thunderstorm cleans me too, from everything I know is wrong yet still stand by.
I pray this bending palm tree inspire me to stand by me, my faith, resisting, yet not quite falling.
I pray this thunderstorm destroy all those who seek to destroy.
I pray to realize a paradox; I pray the thunderstorm not come for me.

With a little bit of a wimpy background, this poem essentially serves an outlet to describe my experience on a cool night, where the ice-cold wind of relief from the AC mixed with the faint, sophisticated smell of aloe vera from a moisturizer. Yet, the feelings of sophistication and nostalgia which compelled me to simulate situations where I would triumph and be the subject of celebrations is priceless, though the relation lacks logic. It is but only instinct.

Invasion For Liberation

Will I let the fragrant wind occupy my sinuses, my self?
The wind fills liberating, the cool rush seems relieving, the battalions of perfume are stationed,
They occupy, yet I lack the will to fight them back, and so shall you.
Instead, I beg them to stay, to make me feel more, to not leave.

Invade and infiltrate to filter out, and free me,
From the shackles of charmless, dull and unimpressive monotony.
Let the aloe vera and cold air not leave my side,
And let me not require distance to make the heart grow fonder.

Invade me to liberate me from reality, of impartial emotions,
From apathetic dullness, and take me somewhere where I feel like I'm born to rule.
Born to enchant, born to impress even through my nonchalance.
Come back, nectar of nostalgia, come back, vantage point where all of the past appears sweet.

It's a sad thing, seeing an old friend change. It's sad to see how fast a pure, joyful smile turns into a blank expression, or worse, a scheming smile. It's infuriating, seeing how manipulative someone you thought you knew so well is. This poem is thus a tale of sorrow, and a promise of revenge.

Play-Dough

Maybe a flower has blossomed, yet there is no way to know,
When exactly, how much, for how long, did it sow,
Hope in a field of personal tribulations, and when, and why it shrank,
The warmth gone without informing us, who knows when it got so dank,

Who knows if I must feel happy or sad, black or white or grey or blue?
Who knows when exactly you came and vanished, or if you were even true?
Though your presence was proven, the glide sends shivers,
The ease with which you changed to poles, a meandering river.

Is play-dough your spirit object? Is this your job
To change, to blur borders, the ability to distinguish you rob?
Maybe we do need you, in other aspects as well, but how do you escape?
Maybe I will catch you red handed, outside your shimmery, figurative cape.

I see you have taken refuge in a polite smile.
I see I have invoked you, and in a while,
I will catch you, and expose your agile, slippery ways.
I will hold you, for once, accountable to the beholder's gaze.

Yes, I am in awe of the gradual dull of the twinkle, of the slow curve of the lips,
The duty to conform to an unwritten, unseen yet very alive law, out it seeps,
As said countless times, slowly but surely, the lips straighten to their dull, boring fate,
To fade with a silent, yet very present pop, like a whirlpool of joy on it's last breath.

Maybe I am supposed to be jubilant, yet I never realized as well,
That triumph was shadowed by regret, and lethargic wistfulness has swelled.
I wonder why, I wonder how and when, have I changed so,
The memories of a voluntary, rare show of all things good in the world linger, my dear play-dough.

This poem aims to deplore and highlight the somewhat realistic dystopia human society seems to sometimes aim towards. The poem cries in despair at some of the apathy and inconsideration some of humanity has come to resemble.

Dance Unto Death

How does it feel when every particle of where you stand,
grumble, fall then rise in revolt?
How does it feel when your home feels a house, and every
other place refuse refuge?
How does it feel when wails are ignored with not even a sign
of struggle, no effort to even avert eyes,
Let alone help the poor moaner with bare bones and
bloody sinews?

Sometimes the quite lips and mannequin eyes scream uglier
than pain.
It feels like the bugs are taking over, when a wish of a good
day goes unheeded,
Ears don't twitch, eyes don't avert from the new, bright
hypnotizing invader.
A little calf may retch and beg in its agonized moos to lift
the tyre trampling its life, the same thing the passerby's, in
essence, lost.

No one stops to think and mourn the life of the innocent bug they squashed for its sake,
No one stops to think about that species, Conscience, which only bugs them nowadays,
Just squashing every fellow living being to satisfy something unknown, but in vain.
All sense of hunger for even achieving one's own justice has vanished, not even this sorry excuse of work in the name of literature can save the dance unto death.

We often don't even feel a slight, thin thread tracing our skin. We are quite numb to its caress. Just so, we often don't even realize and feel the strings which come attached with some of our opinions and thoughts, which manipulate us to make us believe that those ideas and opinions are our very own.

Voluntary Coercion

A forced deed is frowned upon, and morally wrong,
But a deed committed by own will is applauded, as long as it doesn't harm.
But what if the free will is controlled, forced, with strings attached like a puppet?
What of the will hypnotized, willingly at the mercy of someone else's will?

There is no way to know, the source behind
Those sponsored posts, those happy smiles, promoting products and ideas.
There is no way to know, the source behind,
The accusations of external motivation, the hurled abuses of a puppet act?

We are numbed, rendered unable to even detect the thin threads attached to our body and soul,
Blind to perception, even unable to feel the absence of willingness to perform,
To even detect our aversion to such an action. We are living in a world, where all is voluntary,
But really, all is coercion, we give in to voluntary coercion.

Be it out of charity, love, or even patronizing, condescending knowledge of having some dirt against the other party, we often forgive a mistake without saying so but conveying it nonetheless. The culprit knows that we are aware, and the grateful, furtive, ashamed and submitting glances are sometimes what we yearn for.

You and I Know

A knowing glance and an embarrassed one convey enough of a story,
A grudging apology and a patronizing notice of mercy which contains demands of hefty tributes,
Are exchanged, with guilt and gusto and a little bit of rage.
The usually hilarious comedy has turned to tragedy, when the audience is non-existent, and players only two.

A little game of dignified begging, and painful pondering has started.
A silent negotiation of compromises and ruinous demands run to and fro.
A year of guilt, a lifetime of taunts, a kilo of apologies with genuine emotions to be compensated.
Yet secret contempt against the judge is certainly not expected, for criminals must bear the brunt of being grateful.

What a sorry world, where the guilty stop feeling guilty and instead grateful towards a forgiving victim.
What a sorry world where the wronged only seek to wrong more as vengeance, and participate in a cycle of sin.
A childish yet innocent sense of humor turns to a scene of shame when the accidental culprit is clearly alone,
You and I know who is who, yet the elevator doors are closed to everyone else.

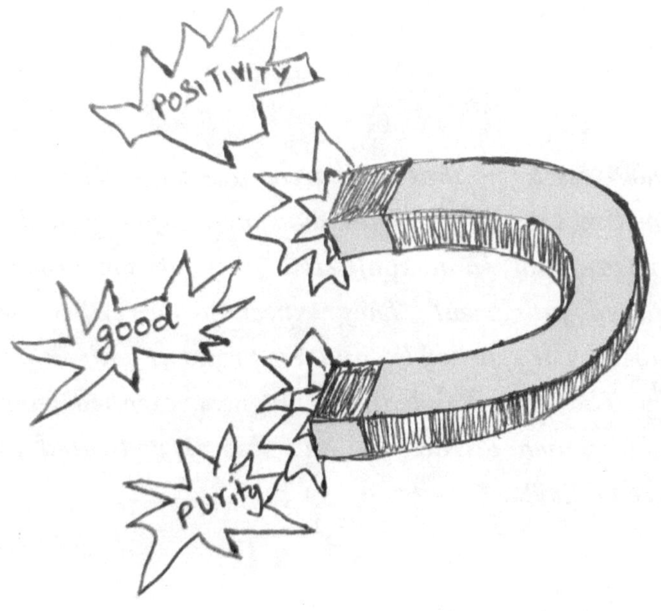
POSITIVITY
good
PURity

Sometimes I feel that grey areas are too celebrated. Sometimes we do yearn for someone unapologetically partisan, not in a conflicted state of somewhere between judgement. They expect to be either be craved by or repelled by, and are proud of both either way. They are the clear-cut magnets, escaped from limbo, which attract us, and this is dedicated to these magnets.

Magnet

Such is a pure magnet, gleaming with two poles,
Clear, proud, visible, opinionated.
Such is a pure magnet which attracts the genuine, repels the evil, and ignores the ambiguous,
A side it itself possesses and is ashamed of, but chooses not to hide it.

Such is a magnet which everyone yearns for but no one deserves,
The one which attracts the true and good, no matter how many, yet has place for them all.
A magnet in which the poles act in unison, yet do not seek to compete,
Such is a magnet which would win the jealous, enemies and hearts, a magnet which would win.

A simple article of everyday use will be missed when lost,
It will be reminisced without regard for how queer it sounds,
To miss a magnet. Yet it is only the metaphorical lessons it leaves behind,
Which will be hopefully savored. Not the magnet, but the role model would be looked up to.

do you
REMEMBER?

Like the name, I treat this poem as a reminder to me, of what I like now and what I shall yearn for later on. It is a manuscript wherein I write of the tangible and intangible which I yearn to visit.

Post-It Notes

I strive to adorn this screen/paper with squiggly little lines,
Which simply refuse to do justice to the power the
memories hold over me,
The grandeur the bright, worshipped thoughts, the
gleaming polish
Which blinds all doubts on hoarding these thoughts, yet
also preaching some.

I write of the warm embrace of my mother, whose warmth
melts away,
A day of cold, frigid, undeserved apathy, animosity, gives
reason to a reasonless day.
I write of the words of acid which try to pulverize the filth I
possess, the taunts shielding me and others from evil.
I write of the imaginary, yet very real, tangible world we
created and share, of little pawns, their lives controlled by us..

I write of the endlessly, forever excited, happy yell my father
makes after a long day away,
I write of the hypocritical longing for jokes I roll eyes at, yet
yearn their speaker when we are away.
I write of the "I told you so" I despise, yet take pride in too,
just like I take pride in what its speaker suggests.
I write of the proud admission that he isn't a sage, yet
admire the sagely wisdom he sprouts.

I write of the dream which woke me up from an afternoon nap,
I write of the kindness I received, I write of chivalry, which, fortunately, still lives.
I write of the sight that inspired my masterpiece, I write of the abyss of darkness I fell into, which no one else can treat, yet I overcame.
I write of my bleeding eyes, yet sane and genuine smile due to the bright side of the world.
I write of the shame I experienced, and the lesson to never repeat anything which shall cause such consequences.

I write of those who fail to see the beauty in either the pleasantly flawed, the flawless, good or bad, or anything at all.
I write of the strange ones who are quick to judge based on parameters which make sense only to them, and should not make sense to anyone,
For that shall be the cesspool where humanity, it's morals and essence are fully drowned, from an inescapable prison of inky evil.
I write of those who put on a smile despite everything, hold out a hand for the wretched yet innocent, the scapegoat,
Their Excalibur the vices, the prejudice in their hearts, the stone their heart.

I write of bad,
I write of good,
I write of all in between,
Yet I have a feeling, my words were in vain, for these, I realize, are unforgettable.

Why must every wish come with strings attached? I seek to address the wish to have a peaceful, blissful, content life without a damage to conscience, without an inner appeal to do good in return, to be on such a heaven on earth.

The Unconditional Request

Sort out the dark and crooked ones, my
otherworldly winnow.
Let the good ones be long and cherished, like a first-time
ride in a limo.
Though the ones who made you live a life of nightmare, like
a benevolent merchant.
Yet I admit, I don't really know you more than a vague pop
culture reference.

Let me sleep, with a smile on my face I can't see but feel.
Let me enjoy the edges of a blanket covering my toes, and a
conscience clean and empty.
Let me not be curious while knowing I would be hurt,
Let me imagine horrid mythical monsters, yet be thrilled
rather than scared.

Absorb all the nightmares I might have, and take them to
your parents,
Take all their well wishes and sweet yet true talks and
flourish me with them.
Capture those warm greetings and well wishes, that
hospitality regardless of origins,
And bring them to my disposal, my loyal filter, my
lieutenant of double standards, my explorer of foreign,
undeserved pleasures.

Be it an enemy, ally, or even a close friend, a reprimand, a stripping of the ego is enough to give members of our kind a broad smile. Even the best of us, the kindest of us, are not immune to the strange, brutal pleasure of someone else's shame, loss of pride, which often comes as a refuge from the boredom of a long eventless day. Or, even in the most rational and well-wishers among humanity, the smile may be caused by relief, relief to not be in this position. Empathy flares up, but not sympathy, in this case, such is our sadistic nature. However, this smile fades as fast as it comes, or even turns into a horrified grimace, when the reprimand turns to us. The, almost musical, transformation in our faces and souls make our double standards, our instinct change- Like waves.

Waves

I struggle hard to conceal the little curve,
The curve which enjoys the shame, the acidic yells,
On the same colleague with whom, not very long ago, I
shared laughs and gossip.
And now, I relish the slow roast of that companion.

The swim was boring, the water was too warm and plain.
Yet all I needed to refresh myself was a sudden cold and
splash in his side of the pool.
The splash enough to relieve me, fulfill my desire for a little
bit of harmless fun.
Though I doubt I could swim in that engulfing,
breathtaking and suffocating cold, and sigh with relief.

Yet the cold spreads, and the curve abandons me,
For its former master's former companion,
For the sadistic traitor who enjoys the cold which freezes
the dignity I had.
The grimace, the frown is invisible to me, but not to him.
The water and our mouths ripple with waves.

Starting off on a clichéd but nevertheless prominent deplorable situation of life with no demarcations. No schedules, no time, yet no work either. Being in between jobs, in between interests, conflicting emotions, favorites, fights, wars, and even timelines. Such confusion seems often to snatch our individuality, or even makes us hate it. Such transition, such mayhem extends to our souls, and often threats our physical and spiritual wellbeing.

In Between

When the surreal turns to existential crisis, the overdose
is realized.
Of drugs, of monotony, of rushed days.
When the blissful intoxication turns toxic, there is no way out.
In between jobs, in between favours, and there is no way
to escape.

A rare break, a rare holiday is received, which is hellish too.
Trying to converse with the only ones you can trust and
truly love, while on the phone.
And your last bastion of good faith has been obliterated.

Yet there is no way to escape this tug of war,
for another call is on hold,
Holding you back from having a terrible meal of
pickles with pudding.
Moral dilemmas trample you, and try to break you apart,
From yourself. The conscience is hunted, and crushed
like a dead claw.
And you make your last stand. Defeat is imminent.
Divorce from yourself is for sure.
Defend honour, and end it yourself, before something
else does.

Be it opinion articles, which are more open (or blatant, depending on one's personal views) about their motive and opinions, or novels, poems, or any other art form, which are more subtle in expressing their thoughts through subtle symbolism, literature has been, is, and will surely be used as an effective tool to express views be it socio-economic, political, moral or emotional, or even an inside joke. Of course, most pieces of art aren't "partisan" in the political sense, but in every such piece of art, even those shrouded in ambiguity, lies views. And if there aren't, new ones will be interpreted. For some, those words, symbols attack their personal thoughts, while for some, those very words are empowering. A weapon for one, torturing device for another, those curved arrows are always there.

Curved Arrows

You speak with scorn, you speak with hate,
You speak with gross incompetence and incoherence.
You point fingers, a finger which stinks of bigotry and hate.
Your scathing remarks are unsolicited, unwanted, just like you.

I appreciate your honesty. I appreciate your bravery,
In penning down words and painting subtle taunts,
In a prickly world. You said what no one else was allowed to.
You have shown the hypocrites their place, you have been brave enough,
To take on the onus to counter the dominant, the voices which only seek to silence dissidents.

Do all such celebrations of free thought and liberty require to take a side?
Can't a flower be a flower instead of a party flag?
Can't a few words be taken at face value? Can't a storm be understood as a torrent of wind?
Must we always attack, or be attacked, regardless of the justice of the attacks, by these curved arrows?

Be it a slight drizzle, or be it a raging, torrential rain, the earthy smell, the cool, wet wind which showers with love and long-lost memories, happy or heart breaking, is something we all have had the privilege to experience, or hope to, in the parched valley of death. The pleasant greeter of bountiful harvest, however, is also sometimes the harbinger of death, pain, drowning, lack and separation. These very truths exist, are realized, and deservedly discussed. Extensively, must I add. But the metaphorical, the symbolic art of the rain, though, also thoroughly discussed, fails to cease fascinating us, as admirers of literature, and lucky enough to have the basic needs of life met. The aspect of rain which deals with the soul, the emotion, in particular, is an aspect I felt worth delving into more. Thus, I strived to create something which resembles what I felt about the rain as a Cleanser of Souls, as a detergent of sorts, washing away emotions and symbols of pain and lethargy.

Whisk Them All Away with You

All the paper cuts and tears, the blood which has been shed,
May you wash it away, may you make a river of blood, but
away from us.
All the pain, all the yells, the agony, the salty tears,
May you whisk them away, take away their parasitic, acidic,
mirthful drift.

I invite you to the mouth of the parched, to the wretched
yet innocent dweller,
Of hellfire, of sandy dystopia. Introduce purity to us.
It's a word I have heard, but none of us have
experienced any more.
Wash away the congealed blood of fellow beings, siblings.

Take away the breath we have been holding on for so long,
allow us to finally inhale.
With a smile on our face instead of a mask. Take
away the toil,
The burden on our backs, heads, conscience, and soul.
Whisk away the sweat, the blood, the tears, the sludge of
deceit. Whisk them all away with you.

Adrijaa

Self-pity, shame, guilt and sometimes most profoundly, exhaustion. The will to just get over with it, to submit to the invincible cause, be it just or unjust. What goes on in us, when we finally submit? When do we want to feel together, solidarity in defeat, yet feel alone? What happens to the humbled, is what I try to explore.

I Submit

Even for lips to quiver, energy is needed, something I don't possess,
Something drained in this long, useless, pointless war to prove a point.
A point I lost, we lost, they lost, somewhere along the way,
Somewhere, sometime during those stabs and dismemberment and conspiracies.

Even to protest and argue, we must know what we stand for, and what they stand for too.
Something we don't remember, along with our values and morals.
For all is lost in this unjust defeat.
Now we must pay, while battling within myself to fight the shame welling inside, and try to not show it.

The wounds to the skin will go away, but not the pride.
The tissues shall regenerate, but not the lost glory.
We are sorry, I am sorry. Where have I and we descended?
We huddle together in prisons, yet the cold seeps in anyways, the ghosts still haunt.

It's a dreaded cause of extreme discomfort, stomach cramps. They pain where you can't even look, and when they stop for even a moment, the relief is immeasurable. What was normal and ordinary before seems heavenly and extraordinary. And when we start to feel a little too cosy, a barrage of attacks on the innocent belly rains again. And we think: what have we done to deserve this? Why us? Similar is the case of the world in which we live in. It changes, for both the worse and the better. What was normal then, is out of the ordinary now, be it fortunately or unfortunately. The constant animosity, the bloodshed, the thirst, the aversion to be civil is constant, somewhere or the other, and in us too, yet we can't really point out why, why does it have to be that way? Yet, for even a fraction of a moment, an act of kindness, selflessness by a stranger is committed just because, there seems to fall a blanket of humanity, long forgotten. A cease-fire, the mere absence of constant rifle shots and booming cannons for even a day is cherished. It's an enigma, why and how, the world cramps.

Stomach Cramps

Why must the cannons be aimed at the soft underbelly?
Why must you prove yourself a coward, and not
show your face?
You, who have caused all things wrong with me and
everyone else, for no fault of ours,
Or if we are more guilty than we think, then why don't you
enlighten us?

You, who feed on me, and attack where I can't even see you,
But only feel the agony, and only wonder why do you
bother to do so?
Why do you want to go to war, why do you want
to conquer?
What do you have to prove to yourself, by eliminating all else?

What do you feel when you expel, antagonize, persecute,
and torture,
For no reason at all. And what do you expect,
From those you trod upon, from those who are visibly red
from anger and tragedy?
Why did you start this cycle of pain, why won't you behave?
It would only cost you your evil, that's it.

How do you manage to subjugate, and prevent us from rebelling?
You stop your evil clutch just long enough,
For us to experience the ecstasy, which was normal not long ago, and forgive,
And start clutching again. Yet you also sink hope, false or otherwise, apart from those gnarly nails.

Circumstances drive us to irritation, frustration, anger, and sometimes to the point of self-pity and sorrow. What is worse, to our selfish souls, is that we find no one to blame except ourselves and the circumstances. We go to great lengths to invent new crimes and assign them to imagined culprits, yet never find closure. We try to divert ourselves to antagonize and fantasize about an external enemy, but our souls aren't a dictatorship requiring gullible minds to not rebel and side with the dictator, for our conscience is but only one. We are the dictator, or the gullible, frustrated. We keep on alienating, but the more rational ones among us apologize to the wronged, and blame themselves, the circumstances quietly, and accept, that we are, in fact, embroiled in a civil war. A war, with our own self.

War with Oneself

The explosions, the bombs one deserves but doesn't want,
hurts oneself sorely.
The constant itch, the constant ruffle of the hairs of one's
leg by belligerent fighter jets,
Only there to suck one out, like a parasite.
There is no pain, but slight discomfort. Yet the inner self is
brutalized.

Moral dilemmas which no one caused on intention, yet one
is embroiled in it.
The enemy is invisible, non-living, yet lurking, but no one
you know or around you.
Yet one lashes out and attacks everyone else who isn't a
stakeholder,
In the constant, soft, blood-curdling, gradual drip of cold
water on one's hair.

Why spew acid on those who seek to remedy, instead of the
enemy which lies within?
Why blame all except one's own self? Why itch the skin,
when it's the intrinsic passions which itch?
Why wrench an innocent bystander's hands from each
other, instead of the guilty conscience, the apology which
wants to be free?
Why declare war on anyone else, when the war is with oneself?

We just wait, hunching in anticipation, waiting impatiently for our subject of interaction to hang up the phone. Yet we don't dare to throw the phone away, or even interrupt them, to not risk a relationship getting destroyed, or annoy the one we need a good mood to be in, or simply, just because we are civil. But in these gut-wrenching moments of anxiety before confessions, request, or conveyance of a matter of urgency which we just let wait, we do what we hate, we commit the ultimate feat of waiting to not ruin the relationship, and in the process, we come to detest our subject. For we, I am sure, are quite familiar with the angst one feels when we found or recalled something of utmost importance and interest to us and them, and just when we squeak, so does the bloodcurdling, nasal ring of the phone. Little do we know who are they talking to, about what, and how much more important, crucial is that call than our own matters of importance. Here is an ode to what we sense, when we witness someone on a call.

On A Call

We have held our breath in, we held our feelings, our tears,
our laughs in, and the burden on our conscience.
Yet now, the confession can't wait, the words flood the guilty
mouth and threaten to shoot out like projectiles,
Hurting me, and hurting you, causing you to squeal on
the phone.
Yet I don't want to be the rude interruption, don't want to
disappoint even more.

How about you buy me this, or allow me that, my dear, my
sweet, my precious?
Is what I thought of asking, with a preceding storm of
favours to you.
Yet the sugar trap fell to no avail, or to a frustrating delay,
my engineered trance ruined with a shrill, blasting shriek.
The little piece of metal has wrapped you into its cold hard
body! But I still won't risk my chances.

It is an interesting proposition, something to ponder upon,
something only we are interested in.
What's that? Another call? Never mind. I forgot. Must be
an important, interesting conversation.
Yes, my words, or rather unspoken thoughts stink of
sarcastic taunts. Yet I see no point in abandoning my civility,
To snatch something belonging to someone I love and respect.

Let me take on the burden of waiting, to not risk and ruin it.
And in the process,
My own back has broken. I have in fact ruined my own feeling of interest and attachment.
Chat to your heart's content, with whoever who turns your frown to a smile after hanging up.
A pained smile, a smile of veil, I realize, as guilt washes over, veiling the bad news to put on a brave face for me.

Our protagonist, in this situation, is not someone who should seem to deserve sympathy in his circumstances, if seen from an outward perspective. Yet he is just as much in danger as someone who doesn't get what they deserve, even after years and decades and lifetime of toil. He is drowning in donations, luxury, and shame. He is rendered mute by those who choose to not hear his appeals to stop these undeserved showering of worldly pleasures. He is seemingly given everything, but deep inside, he knows everything is snatched from him: his pride, his right to achieve, his sense of achievement, his chance to work hard for the fruit, to be one of them, one of those who deserve the esteemed salutations and delicate silverware after years of toil. He may be drowning in chocolate, but he's drowning nonetheless.

Call for Help, Drowning in Chocolate

He calls for help, but only bubbles come out, as more chocolate is poured,
More caramel, more sweets, more macaroons are dipped, and left for him to consume.
He is cursed with slurs, he is called "mister" and "sir".
All his attempts to use his hands to escape are swatted, with sweet wishes showering more sweets.

He can see the decadence, ruining him and his soul,
Yet he can't call for help, he can't cry.
The tears are sweet as well, he wants to be reprimanded.
He doesn't want to dip low hanging fruits; he wants to escape this cursed fountain of luxury.

He wants to lash out against a world, who didn't show him its usual cruelty.
He wants to lash out against those who snatched his satisfaction to work to deserve, yet he can barely do so.
His conscience is a burden, he wants to be compensated,
For there is no lifeguard, no guardian to beat some sense to him, to rescue him. He calls for help from a cruel fountain of chocolate.

The Great Middle, a place where I believe most things, phenomena, and issues belong. The vast majority of everything everywhere, I believe, is inconspicuous. Most people, they believe, are doing just okay. Most things we outgrow fast, most of what is produced in the world is mediocre, and most souls go to a place and "live" an afterlife they have no strong feelings on. Yet this great mediocrity is not necessarily something to be ignored, to let go unnoticed. This great mediocrity, I feel, is also a cause for awe, merely for its large dominion.

The Great Middle

The sewers are shunned at, villainized, and the destruction of poverty and utopia yearned for,
Vilified and admired respectively, and rightfully so.
There is more evil than good everywhere, with exceptions and differing margins.
Yet all are blind to the translucent shadow their overlord casts.

All voyagers who sojourned from the land of the miserable to the delighted, have forgotten about the apathetic,
The land which felt infinite, which snatched their energy to travel.
All my superior scribes and masters of language, words, shapes and colours,
Have succeeded in failing to even notice the vast mundane, which occupy all except the margins of their eyes,
But dominate their horizons and soul.

Most flowers seem without fragrance, not all weed parasitic travesty on nature,
Most expressions are blank, regardless of what one feels.
And that is but natural, instead of a conscious effort the veil true sensation.
The understated, vast, tremendous Great Middle smack in front of everyone, but invisible to most.

There are quite a few things, phenomena, attitudes in which it is hard to detect where they changed and when. What went wrong, what is exactly different from before, they are never sensed. Everything seems the same on surface, if each little cog is seen individually. Yet the "different" sensation is quite distinct in the bigger picture. When did a child grow apart from the parents? When did active obsession turn to heart wrenching apathy? Who was the secret killer who took away these little miracles back then? Surely, it's graduality, the sly weasel wearing the mask of a wise turtle who only seeks to give peace of mind. And it is the wisest sloth I, or maybe we, have ever met.

The Wisest Snail I Ever Met

What makes us hungry, and what is different then,
Then when we are satiated?
Or it just a new curiosity, or anxiety, or gluttony,
And what separates them?

Who tells us we are sad, and how is it different,
From when we feel our usual, bland apathy?
The same blank expressions go a long way,
Unless lips quiver and rivers of tear flow, though when did the hidden ice melt?

Why do we wince when are legs are hammered, why utter the terrible shriek?
And who decides what is bad and why?
And is bad, negative, pain and evil, to be repelled by
And if so, why?

There were no quarrels, there were no shudders of disgust,
None noticeable at least, though when did you part?
When was the moment we loosened the bond which held us together?
When was the taut bond eaten away, loosened, and now on its last few strings?

When did the rations become so dismal, yet we failed to notice?
When did the flood of soup discreetly became a sorry, scummy pond?
It was right in front of us. When did the sun set? I was looking at it all day.
I'm blind to realization. Answer me the reasons, and how you did what you did, o snail,
The wisest snail I ever met.

The best piece of work, art anyone has ever done. The only chance a mere mortal has to immortality. The only chance a slighted, fallen human has to get up for once, in a last, heroic stand against disrepute and mediocrity haunting oneself for quite a while. The last chance to defend the petty yet necessary human concept: honour and dignity. The Magnum Opus is all that and more. It must be gaped at, with wide eyes from supporters and the apathetic, and begrudgingly from opponents and villains of one's life. The Magnum Opus must be the life; if the life is magnanimous, it must resemble all that and more, if it's banal and ordinary, the Magnum Opus presents the last chance to be true that banality while dazzling the easily bored. Luck is wished, though your honour demands to really only on the talent one takes pride in, and give it all up for one's last stand at the life of art, the Magnum Opus.

The Rulebook for a Magnum Opus

I have fallen into the pit of irrelevance, the same place where i was born,
And spent many happy, blissful days there, in that cold, damp place, shielding me from hot passion,
Up there, in the bright, glittery ground, which I admired from a distance, but wasn't tempted by,
Until I strained my muscles and sinews to reach the ground, and felt the warm air of obsession, hands begging to shake mine.

I was told by a shooting star to follow it in its celestial land,
To dart like it, to be like it, to shine brighter than and run faster than it,
And leave a wake of destruction on the way for a surely worthy cause, if need be.
Yet the supernova was misleading, burning me, leaving behind a pile of ashes looking down upon wronged mortals
Who not so long ago, gave me a rope to hoist myself to where I am now.

I cannot repent, for I shall not be pushed to more shame,
I shall not be any more of a traitor to my people and my former maenads,
And my being identity, which is anything but humble now.

Deviation would only lead to exacerbation, apologies,
no matter how much I wish to offer them, shall only
lead to shame.

I can only spite them, to the point of adoration.
I can only insult them enough for them to grudgingly
respect my rise, peak, and fall.
I shall be cornered by my own actions, be wallowing in
self-pity,
Yet put that behind a veil of stone-faced moral ambiguity.

I shall look into the star, in its pure, hard core, and implode,
But into fireworks. I shall be the horror which haunts their
life, yet they avert their eyes and mind either.
I shall make a spectacle of my end, I shall be terrible, but i
shall be etched.
My last stand must be etched in disgust, fear, awe and
admiration.
My ashes shall caress all onlookers, blanket them, like
pepper on meat, and thus, shall be my Magnum Opus.

U
N
I
T
Y

Maybe a little cliché, but the ideal of unity in diversity is what this poem appreciates. The pointlessness of hating those different from you, the parochial view of maintaining homogeneity for the sake of it confounds this poem.

Fly Away

Fly away, o burden to my people, you long-beaked freaks,
Your pinkish throat, your call which makes a symphony as it mixes with the others,
Must be severed and muted. Your long, thin legs, your appearance,
Must not pollute the pristine uniformity of my land.

Fly away, o black tailed one, a threat to the existence of my people
Is your mere existence. Yet our strength shall trample you, or make you flutter away,
To your boreal frigid lands. Then no longer shall you threaten,
The fragile existence of our pure, invincible kind.

Who would have known that they shall woo those who I swore to defend,
Lured by their color, to a land where such gross deviance is celebrated?
Who would have known, I would be left alone,
Amidst only the caws of a sea of black?

A puppet without being aware of itself, walking and fighting yet not feeling anything, losing wars, loved ones and peace of mind yet not feeling anything at all, be it psychotic glee yet natural remorse, constantly steeped in apathy. Only caring and looking out for oneself, yet selfish doesn't quite sum it up, for one doesn't know why or when one stopped caring for others, and it's a fact which causes one neither guilt, nor joy, for one is merely apathetic, loss and gain is not felt. Such is what seems to be our world in my eyes, now. There are very few aggressions yet also very few who convey solidarity, few who push someone into a rushing train yet few who strive to save the shoved. Such an invisible King seems to rule the world, and apathetic is this great, numb King.

Numb King

Don't you see, my lord, your legs are paralyzed from the last
war against Lonesome,
Yet don't you wonder, my lord, how do your legs move,
like a fallen script thrown on rapids, tarnished with single,
discreet tear?
Don't you see, my lord, that the mirror greets you with the
image of a statue, yet your limbs move in inhumane perfection?
Don't you see, my lord, the lack of rage, sorrow, ecstasy,
innocence, guilt, life and motive in you, yet your dominion
still goes on?

Only your limbs move, your heart pumps, your
mouth dances, yet your eyes are without life, your skin
abandoning utility.
And thus you rule the same way you are ruled, ruling over
subjects who are, but barely.
Your family, companions, commanders, courtiers are taken
away and reduced to clay dolls,
The crown jewel you cherished has been snatched, your
silken, stately robes have been burnt, yet your lips don't
quiver. Your glassy eyes merely reflect the flame.

The same flame which once burnt inside you, inside your
grey character and active heart, the flame of passion,
The flame of hatred, bigotry, rage, love, affection,
community hearth which once used to mar your land, your
bittersweet dominion,

Has been extinguished, and only apathy rules now, there is no one to harm but no one to save, no words of insult yet no true compliments.
And I don't know how to feel about this, for I am numb too, I feel neither satisfied nor disappointed, for your faithful chronicler is also numb, King.

A cult of a personality, back then, is barely noticed now. A saviour, a messiah back then is just a man wearing a torn, redundant cape, reminiscing the past to whoever bothers to listen. There was a time when everyone flocked to hear this man speak and be hypnotized by those words willingly. Now, however, each shout is avoided, the yell, the simulation of those speeches are now dismissed as the ramblings of the senile, though with good reason. His joints pain now, he's frail body requires support, for he can no longer carry the hopes, aspirations, admiration of a whole nation on his back, he can no longer rescue anyone, he can no longer rush to save the innocent from a fire, for he himself is out of breath. He was on a hiatus, which invited sorrow and requests to reconsider, but turned to apathy. And now that he's back, in an underwhelming gait, we all wish it was more than a hiatus. We all wished that he left when the flowers were still showered on him, he left in utmost grace as the flowers eventually cover his formerly majestic view, and thus, never make the underwhelming return, never come back.

I'm Back, But.....

The cape is muddy, and it's red colour fails to camouflage the dry blood it spilled,
Yet I shall wear it once again, my fans don't believe in heroes without one.
My admirers are true admirers, and shall excuse the lack of a chiseled, sculpted exterior.
They shall surely overlook the frail body covered by the cape, which engulfs it.

They shall, after all, expect a God which returned, after a long, mirthless vacuum of presence.
They shall break out of their reverie, they shall stop avoiding my glance, the moment they can't hold the flood of emotions they feel at my sudden appearance,
And they shall cave in to the charisma I still hold, and I shall reprimand them,
For the childish, clichéd pretense of ignorance and a subsequent service in honour of the pranked, is getting old.
Except that my own patience had given way, and I forced myself on to the highest pedestal of the town square,
Yelling at my worshippers, who walk past me with disgust in their faces, covering their children's ears.

Me, who saved them from all the evil which plagued this miserable town,
From the new, alien heathen which tried to invade this cursed town,
By their mere presence. There was a time when my fiery speeches attracted all those who lived,
A few words from me were enough to incite them against their own, and the heathen insects which crawled over the place.

Yet my throat can be clear for only so long, and I had to leave, amid showers of flowers,
And appeals and requests and shrieks and cries begging me to stay back.
Why must I heed your requests now, to save the little girl drowning in the fountain right beside me?
My back has gone, my arms ache, my pride is wounded, I should be saved instead.

When one hole is blocked, another one opens, and the water spurts out with an intent to hurt with its blade-sharp surface as soon as it can escape and stab the very beings it provides life force to. At the same time, when all hope seems lost, when all goals seem to be rendered futile, when all missions fail successfully, new avenues and opportunities arise. When ten assignments are finished, twenty more arise, a hundred soldiers are killed, a thousand more are convinced to replace them, when sunshine seems to be everywhere, clouds float and prove otherwise, when droughts in the field, soul and creativity seem to be the norm forever, a single drop of water, hope, closure, eureka signal the compensatory flood. We feel we hate the noise, yet as humans, our innermost consciousness craves human presence, with it's imperfection but also the warm nectar of humanity unique to us, and our race has gone to great lengths to protect this humanity, this bustle in the arcade of the world. Quite like a whack-a-mole, destruction of something good or evil seems to result in the abundance of the very phenomena, events, emotions seemingly destroyed. It is not an enigma why; I feel it is merely the rules of universal balance and justice taking its course.

Whack-A-Mole

Why must you show your ugly, smug whiskered face each
time I hammer you to death?
Why must you of all beings, possess the camaraderie we
could never have?
What have you done to deserve it anyway? All you do is
frustrate my kind,
And leave us to vent out the anger to those who don't
deserve it.

Why is there no scar on your face and soul and past, unlike
quite a few of us?
Why must you smile at us? Your sadistic kind takes joy
in our pain.
May you be broken one day, you and all those who
replace you.
Let there be none of your kind left, no one to save you or
your deformed, broken face. And then I shall gleefully laugh.

Yet there seems to be a miserable silence, a lonesome time I
thought would be my moment of closure,
Of peace, of ecstasy. Yet the it is haunting, it is despairing,
for there is nothing to left to play, to do, to see,
look forward to it.
No longer plays the stereotypical game music, no longer
does the chaotic crowd of enjoyers sing their terribly sweet
song of joy,

Of convivial times, of times when human empathy, solidarity existed, when human voices persevered through times of hoarse throats.

And then the lights spring back on, so do your heads, greeting us with a knowing, sympathetic smile. You seem to know when to spare us from taunts.
Thank you for your mercy, your lack of change in behavior, the lack of words, but the rush of relief.
Thank you for letting me know that I am not alone, or, thankfully, WE aren't.
Thank you for indulging me without making me wear of the look on my face, the rush on my mind. Thank you, crowded and bright arcade. Thank you, whack-a-mole.

Everything around is disgusting and heartless. The flies seem to cause disease and bite as well. The hard earned wages are squandered in wagers and liquor, and companions, once soul mates are thrashed. The one thing which all can afford, and is for free, is ridiculed at, those who require it are termed insane and dealt with. The flames bouncing on to the workers' bare skin in the scrap metal warehouse is stared at, not with awe and appreciation, but for jeering and the amazement at the supposed inferiority of the exotic. Let's seek to explore what such squalor shall, or does, look like.

Squalor

The fleas don't seem to forgive the immobile dog, though the reason is unknown,
The dog just faces more torment and starvation, and the taunt of the fleas.
The penniless, stateless, yet heathen widow is a "fortune seeker", say the suited investment bankers,
"They" are a "flock", we are a "pride", "they" try to snatch a history from "us", when there was only "us".
And thus begins a hunt to violate the witch. Thus commences the stabs and piercing of wombs, laced with acidic taunts; you will never belong, subhuman.

Little kids with wild eyes, frizzy hair and muscles as hard as iron,
Lost dignity in a world with no safe zone, no one to provide for them, no means to even grab,
Yet they are scammers in the eyes of all, these children with sunken eyes and ribs, cloth and childhood torn to shreds, they are a dangerous gang of thieves.

The one who lost all, yet still has to lose so much, receives paparazzi each day,
Not like a superstar, but an object, of pity, poverty, shame, to be jeered at.
The flames hit his bare skin, yet the flames which hurt him are invisible, they are only audible.
Such is a dystopia, a farfetched story of squalor, a fantasy.

Classified government documents exist even in the most democratic countries. Insincere promises are delivered by politicians even to an audience hardened by experience, through powerful rhetoric. Inflated tales of valour and goodness are broadcasted by all, everything is transparent to the jubilation of the stakeholders, except that the transparent screen is in fact, a movie, fake footage of deception. The exchange of money, expressions and values is quite invisible, though one can still see, not through the screen but the screen itself. Such is the world of graceful deception we choose to live in and admire, the exquisite mosaic of dishonesty and deception.

Mosaic

The fountain of youth isn't in a clandestine forest or swamp,
It is merely concealed from our souls, by the curtains
of our mind.
The goodness in humanity isn't rare, it is merely gagged,
It is separated from humanity by a mosaic wall, enough for
us to ignore.

The explosions of passion, red hot rage, green envy,
Cruelty, dark evil and crimson blood,
Flowing like a humongous serpent, all happen behind
the mosaic.
Yet it seems like a magnificent, graceful display of fireworks,
enough to invoke awe.

The CCTV is on loop, the drugged residents are
satiated anyways.
The guards are strong and alert to protect the dirty
strangers who are the thieves.
But what if the thief wears silk coats, a Nehru cap, and a
charming smile?
Is there any way to know that these aren't stolen or
snatched? is there any way to know if it's a window or
mirror? Is there any way to break the spell of the mosaic

A heroic fiction, a ride through a fairy tale, a strange, surreal life in the Wonderland where Alice stumbled on; of course, they are stories and we are quite aware of it. Yet, if an escape to a game where we ourselves are the heroes of our scenarios instead of the constant victim of verbal abuse from bosses and "superiors" is what it takes to survive, so be it. If a refugee to a new world where everything is ideal according to us is what we are at the literal end of the day, to make the real world more sense and less brutal, then let us wander so. If we are the best of the orators and minions of justice to escape from a world where the one who has wronged did not receive poetic justice, then why not escape so? The few times the jelly in our skull is put to use and is thus appreciated (though by ourselves) is when it is a scenario simulator, when it helps us forget trauma through woven utopia which is dystopia for some, and might even be contradictory, when it helps us forget embarrassment through a heroic, chic, alternate reality. Follows an account of just another scenario I would ideally want to be in, yet can only simulate.

Scenario Simulator

I live in Utopia, a cottage on a rolling, green hill,
It is surrounded by rolling meadows and poultry and sheep
and low wooden fences.
It is free of sin, it is pure bliss, it is small, yet
No one feels claustrophobic.
It's corners never see time-outs, it's quaint little windows
only see the sunshine,
The lively boughs of nurtured trees, the beauty of the world.
No one need leave. My reality is the reality of the world.

I ride a Vespa through a spotless, winding aisle,
My only audience are palm trees bending in reverence,
In quite pride, swaying ever so slightly, in mirthful sorrow.
They shall miss me later. They seem to nod, as I kiss the
sun, the briny breeze,
With no one to object, nothing to object to my incompetence,
my tardiness, for no consequence waits for me.

I go to a posh hill station for the final session of a
prestigious summit I am worthy enough to attend,
On my own merit. I am lodged in a cozy cottage overlooking
lofty, rugged, heartless, freezing mounds shrouded in dark,
Hot chocolate on my palm, blanket on my body and feet
pointing to the hearth.
And I spot my old friends among whom I was a success,
huddling around the bonfire.

One of my comrades strumming the guitar, though the
voice comes from the heart instead of the mouth.

I rush discreetly, shush the astonished, and quickly borrow a violin,
And join him. A sad instrument, though now the tears
which do come out, are of joy, of nostalgia.
The goosebumps are there, the shiver is visible, but none
due to the cold.
Strumming hands and waving sticks reunite for a doublet
none of us shall forget.
Two sounds wave as one, two hearts sing as one, a crowd
sing as one.

The spectacle shall hold the attention of every guest and
every one of my naysayers.
We shall throw the banana peel stuck on our shirts since
when we tried to join conversations into the fire.
We shall throw the rude rebuke to the polite offer of help
into the fire,
We shall throw the filth of intolerance and dehumanization
in the fire,
We shall throw the hate of others, other voices, the new
into the fire,
We shall throw the whip against dissent into the fire,
We shall throw those who disagree into the fire,
As we strum and wave the night away, as the crowd sings
with us, laugh not at but with us, the fire sway to our
melody, as it rages with us.

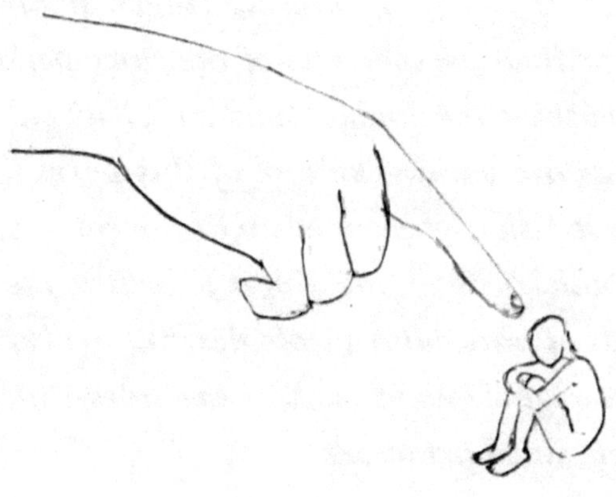

This poem is merely a pointing finger. It highlights the hypocritical perspectives of the same person, yet, though mocking the double standards, both sides, both arguments are valid. The aim of this poem is not to belittle a selfish argument or an argument of begging, or even both. Instead, the aim is to belittle the double standards of particular ideologies, but to also uphold the valid arguments of each of the sides which form it's double sided principle.

Blame

Why must I share, or rather, rot what I have earned?
Why must I extinguish those who want burn?
Why must I bear the brunt of a burden I didn't create
And I be accused of a cold heart and a preacher of hate?

Aren't you the evil one, who revel in sweet talks of acceptance,
Yet turn grim as sudden as you dump your own sense,
Of principle, of righteousness, when the groups are merely
interchanged,
You, yes you, who label those who disagree as deranged?

A thousand fingers point at you, though you see none.
Your kind, and all those you represent, don't you always run?
When a little poof blows your way, your wings flap,

And when a new, richer master you spot, your tails wag!
You growl and spew poison, on those who don't conform,
Yet bleat when the rebels will surely storm
Your bastion, unless you yourself don't surrender,
Such burdening creatures, you serpents, the bane of menders!

Why can't I get more than my measly wages from the
factories you own?
Why must I make do with my paltry income, while you
enjoy what I have sown?
Why must you, yes you, who are responsible for my
indebted, mortgaged, ransomed case,

Shy away from giving up a tiny bit your net 'worth', and brighten up my days?

Why must your, yes your hateful selves, who have inherited your worth, forget about the debt,
You cold hearted ones also undeservedly made part of your treasure, after your forefather's death?
The debt from us which we, I have loaned, or rather coerced to do so,
Why must I flounder in this acidic lake, this inferno of woe?

One of the main appeals of gorging on fiery chillies, tearing up and cackling simultaneously like a sadistic hyena, is pain. This typical definition of evil is something which is secretly desired by our primal selves. The extreme discomfort is the bane of our beings, and also our blessing in the form of negative reinforcements, punishing and pushing us back to our right ways, also giving a stinging, painful, pleasure, the capacity for which was unbeknownst to us. Let us celebrate that pain we deserve and sometimes, crave. Let us celebrate that held breath.

Hold That Breath

I challenge you to hold your breath, a challenge with
transcends it's childish, banal connotations,
I challenge you to hold it, until you feel like you
want to drown,
Until you revel in its pain, the pain inflicted by your captor,
Your own incompetence at even choosing a battle, a patient
of Stockholm Syndrome.

Hold that breath, as a challenge, until you fulfilled your
obligations,
The drowsy, induced illusions, only serve to mellow your
lazy, procrastinating self,
Those vivid illusions shall serve as reminders, as deterrents
from postponing,
Maybe learn to appreciate the tough love, of holding
your breath.

Hold your breath until you can let your thoughts run free.
Hold your breath until you feel you are free,
From the real suffocation of your spirit and mind.
If need be, hold that breath, until you are numb to your
conscience strangling you.

Above and behind the frontbenchers lie the members of a parliament who may have opinions and actual motivation for argument. They may want to genuinely represent and secure benefits for their constituencies, they may want to address their problems, yet time limits and lung power from the front suppresses their voice. Their efforts to speak go unnoticed by rigid heads, and thus, their silence interpreted as incompetency and cause for disrepute. Such is also the case of societal hierarchies, and students, and mates in a friend group. Such is the invisible hand which silences them, their reason, and their motivations and problems. Such is the invisible and ever-widening gap though all peer in and shove and push towards the center. Such is the tyranny of the orbit.

Orbit

The stars favour you in your revolutions to prosperity, in
your bellows to prove your point.
Your lungs are granted the engines of fire, their roar revered,
reverberated everywhere.
Your restless limbs and animated face shed light and make
distinct what you stand for and advocate.
You are able, but also a lucky firebrand, you who are in the
front, for your stand most supported, refuted, but always
reacted to.

Luck is an excuse for the weak, sure. But what of the
Goldilockses who disagree?
Those who get the chance to speak and represent and ask
and advocate, as frequent as a meteor strike?
Yet the disruption to constant disappointment is worth it,
all for the same reception those in the centre of attraction
are used to every day.
The victory is sweet, sweet enough to keep you docile in the
middle, in your usual disappointment.

Then come the trod upon, those who are above all else.
A weak, symbolic, ironic compensation for those who are
prohibited
From self expression in practice. They are above all else, yet
their utterance, grievances fade into the expansive dark,

Of ignorance and deaf ears. Yet the words they utter which are inaudible to all else, is interpreted as incompetent silence.

Stop the tyranny of the orbit, Mr. Speaker, stop the tyranny of the orbit, my king,
I implore you, stop the tyranny of the orbit, Mr. Minister, Mr. President, my leader!
Our pleas, grievances, arguments and opinions mustn't go unheard now, for we are deserving of your consideration,
Unlike the lazy fools in the back who have sewn their mouth shut towards the injustice we face. Free us from this orbit.

When can the volley of work, of arrows, of flames and of sorrow stop? When shall relief in the form of a breeze-laden holiday full of good company and leisurely meals in the backyard show its flawless face and gossamer dress? When shall undeserved insults stop pelting themselves on an innocent, yet inferior and different passerby who just wanted to help the aristocrat who fell into the sewer himself? When shall the acid stop stinging on uncovered, lowered heads and unveiled faces? When shall the homeless, penniless, who left their dignity and human life in their disheveled, frail, wronged, brutalized homelands, stop being shown as aristocratic thieves and fortune seekers deserving only of spite and starvation? When does the flamethrower stop?

Flamethrower, When Do You Stop?

The assignments hurt, they sting my back, they sprain
my muscles,
The promises of no more work broken by "something just
came up" stab my back.
The shooting suggestions and orders fly by with a whoosh,
and break my neck,
Why don't they stop their projectile piercing, and loosen
their suffocating hold?

Slurs are hurled just because, and don't dare to express your hurt,
For you will be hurled with more accusations instead, of
victimizing, of looting the sanctity,
Of a dirty, savage society and system, worth rebelling against.
Help and you shall receive rebukes. Ignore and you shall
be chained, whipped, spit at, made to carry a burden, while
being called one.

When shall those who taunt Samaritans who touch filth to
rescue a fellow fallen being from filth,
Stop? When shall they realize, that they are filthy too?
When shall the flamethrower of ignorance, of bestiality, of
actions and thoughts unbecoming of even the most savage
animals stop?
When shall the flamethrower of destruction, of
degeneration, stop?

Maybe no feelings were meant to be hurt, no taunts and barbs were meant, no incentive to belittle anyone. But if such intentions were in fact present, the perpetrators would be lucky and coy to get away with this seemingly accidental offence: the offence of calling one's namesake. The perked ears turn red as soon as it's stabbed by an "I meant the other person". the days are endured in severe pain, as the namesake, the one you are painfully aware is more important and sought after, is called for several times due to deaf ears busy in catering to their owner's endless fame. The hammer keeps on nailing into your toes, bleeding from envy. Here's to all those with such common names but very different aspirations, personalities, and most of all, essence. Here's to the Roberts and Rahuls of our world

Robert, Rahul

Rahul, Rahul, o Rahul!
Sit down Rahul, I didn't mean you.
And rub that taunting, mirthless smile off your face, sapping the life force of the class.
If only Rahul was here to cheer up the frowns, to lighten the bleak, to save the bored souls, your victims.

No Robert, I didn't call. Never did. It's always the "other" Robert.
You didn't win the scholarship, you didn't win the Best Speaker, the "other" Robert did.
We are still holding our breath for you, especially due to the stench of your mediocrity.
We squint our eyes to look at you, the shadow of your namesake, where you live under, is just too intense.

This is a memorial to the Rahuls and Roberts, invisible for all are blinded by your namesakes.
This is a toast to your endless tolerance for the pain of crushed expectations which pierce your thick skin.
This is a toast to the skill you possess for maneuvering yourself even in the dark shadow of your namesakes.
This is a toast to you, Rahul and Robert, standing strong in the whirlwind of the firebrand behavior and influence, hard to resist.

*Morning walks are refreshing, wholesome, and a breath of fresh air. Walks are supposed to relieve stress, not invite it. Walks are supposed to be in a realm of green and purity, not dust, dung and dirt. Walks are supposed to be times to retrospect, solve mental problems, and create laughably fantastical scenarios where the pedestrian is the victor, the pure, the superior the best. They are not supposed to be times dominated by the frail and old left to fend for themselves in a world which seeks an easy target to crash, they are not supposed to be times when one witnesses emaciated infants thrown into gutters, they are not supposed to be times when one is subject to sights which propel one to seek Nirvana after leaving the material world behind. Thus, us mortals choose to shield our eyes, pucker our mouths, pinch our noses, and continue with the brisk walk. Thus, we, I, continue on this deadly cycle of negligence and squalor.*_

Brisk Morning Walk

My shoes squelch as I step on the moss, my nose twitches in the fresh smell of herbs in their glory,
My eyes squint in pleasant bliss as the sun winks its gentle warmth on my face,
My skin reveling in the joy of the quaint morning, until they shiver,
At the sight of tiny little skeletons with taut skin wrapped over.

The reverie is broken by screeches of infants swimming in filth,
My skin recoils at the touch of their cupped, begging hands.
I slip on dung, I slip on squalor, I bump into migrants of misfortune.
I walk briskly to shield my eyes from the razor sharp rays of the sun.

I do not remember why I strayed into the territory of the alien, the parasitic ghosts.
I do not remember why I bothered to stray, only to hear screams of help and begs.
I do not remember why I considered granting those bony creatures anything, let alone food.
These wretched souls can't be trusted with their own lives, let alone my possessions.

I do not want to waste a morning; I want to take revenge.
On those who snatched my blissful morning, my joy. I shall stray back out again.
Head held high, pushing past the skeletons, letting them fall into the sewers, their homes.
My shoes squelch as I step on the moss, my nose twitches in the fresh smell of herbs in their glory.

It is a solitary confinement, but one voluntary. It is a prison, but a reward instead of a punishment. The Isle of Joy is my little utopia, my little Eden. It is surrounded by an ocean of exclusivity which makes my Isle so special. It keeps out the peasants, the undeserving who destroy the purity.

It's obvious that the idea of a paradise I propose is of course, in reality, quite the opposite. It takes on the idea that even heaven grants itself to all deserving, regardless of the external self. No paradise is true if it excludes, no ideal is worth chasing if it keeps away, deems inferior. My take on a cliché topic worth taking on again and again today, this is my take on the Isle of Joy.

Isle of Joy

My isle of joy is tiny, yet it's sunny and windy and cloudy at the same time.
I'm the parent, the master, the dominant of the Isle.
Nature is me, for I decide the weather, I decide how fluffy the beings shall be.
I shall decide the twilight, the mountains, the plains, the quakes, the eruptions, the fate of livestock.

My Isle is a land of green, green dessert, where my happy cattle feed on.
And they are all happy, or made to look so, or non-existent.
My Isle is visible only when I will the clouds to give in to the Sun, to show my generals the way,
And them. And only them. No other shall step food and pick on the unpicked flowers of my Isle of Joy.

I have a little white cottage with a small white fence which
guards me from the heathen.
The heath shall guard my Isle from the evil, emaciated, hungry,
wretched, penniless fools who seek to break my penance.
Yet the heath seems to grow hostile to all but me, driving
away my loyal companions,
Leaving me by my lonesome, snatching away my joy of my
power over the clouds, water, temperature.
They, you, heath and sea and you lowly mortals, have taken
away my Isle of Joy.

One only yearns a moment of solemn silence to relieve oneself of the 9 hours of burdening, excruciatingly painful, and soulless work. One only yearns silence, and conversation limited to one's own thoughts and self. One yearns relief from children who idolize one, brimming with aimless frenzy and extreme will to talk to said idol, the idol who wishes to be invisible, to hide the face in a last, condescending attempt to face the horde of worshippers. Yet, should one hide face for escape, or in shame, for even contemplating to hide from possibly the only ones one is treated with dignity by the whole day?

Hide Face

Why must I face the gallows of humiliation and negligence and spite all day?
Why must I be made to blacken my face, and wear a garland of clogs,
And paraded all day in infinite insult for each awkward yet inoffensive phrase which sprout from my mouth?
And yet when I be pardoned from the fate of the suffocating chokehold, why must I be grabbed?

Why must I be grabbed by hordes of savages, their dirty hands reaching to touch my feet?
Yes, they are the only ones who treated me with dignity all life, but why must I witness,
Their ugly worship, their ugly sacrifice of their own esteem?
No, I didn't even give it a thought they were merely treating me as an equal instead of a worm, with their honour intact.
Why do you ask?

I need to hide face from the pack of hyenas,
I need to hide face from interaction, and rare words of sympathy.
I need to hide face from the few who worry about its condition,
And how its possessor is doing.

Why must you suggest I hide my face, but with a different
reason altogether?
In shame, in embarrassment, in further spite I deserve to
wallow in?
I disagree. I have most certainly not morphed into those
who mistreated me.
Why, the horde of friends, and family are still there, hurt yet
still asking, "do you need some soup"?

Starry eyed dreams shatter, stars are replaced by tears when the awaited pleasure is cancelled, when the awaited class is cancelled, the awaited engagement is cancelled, the awaited treat is cancelled. Trembling lips and anguished eyes finally start to `relax when the pardon is received, when justice, or rather injustice, is served, when the subject of reprimand is forgotten. A salute and a Salud to such shocks and surprises, which bring disappointment and relief. A cheer sarcastic, and a cheer seriously intended.

Salud

The presentations, the blood my hand shed in writing an epic,
The lectures and sassy comebacks I prepared, forcing heavy eyes open,
Are useless. My eyes are heavy again, but from the burden of a sudden, briny ocean.
There is no war to make a brave last stand on.

There is no peer to triumph over and defeat and break ties with,
No one to jeer at and alienate, all to advocate a minute stand, brutally.
There is no opportunity to shine, and blind even those who helped and rejoiced in my joy.
Salud! To the disappointment which plagues me, for you have won, Salud!

My nausea cannot be concealed, my soul can't be consoled,
Just as the criminal much aware of the gruesome injustice of its crime isn't consoled,
As it trudges to the gallows, with spits and jeers and stones, which are the harbingers of impending doom,
The end of the sum of its life, which it wishes would extend a little more.

I am also aware, and sorry for my crime, and also that I got caught.
I shall not reveal my crime, for I shall save the little dignity I have until later when I shall end,

My joys and wishes and peace of conscience and mind, for good. The frown blasts into a smile too fast,
The pardon, the amnesia has set in! I shall toast a grateful Salud! To my fate!

I shall cheer, either as a slow, mocking clap, or a cackle and a giggle which turns to an ecstatic sob.
I shall cheer, and toast, but I shall not remain quiet, though my noise is unwelcome.
I might, though I don't want to, receive such cheers
(or rather jeers) in exchange,
But I vow and swear and promise to cheer, I promise to Salud!

He lays mulch to protect and keep his soil moist. She spreads her arms, not caring how her joints feels, not caring how much they want to escape, just so her soil can revel in its new-found fertility. They brave the rain, the acid, the casteist and classist slurs to serve their sponsors, the only ones who understand the value of their feeders and the necessity to pander them with what they deserve. this is a tribute to those who know what others deserve, and deliver the same. This is a tribute to their likes.

Mercy, Kotwal

The joints crack, the back aches, yet they continue to bend and spread,
Their exhausted backs, their blistered hands, their tired but braving spirits.
They are called the breadwinners by the family, but they know who they are.
They are called low and burden and village idiots, but they know who they are.

They are spit at by their lenders, yet they shield the acid from reaching the soil,
Their parents, their lands, their providers, the only ones respectful enough,
To not extend their weight, their burden on to the innocent land.
They are innocent, *kotwal,* they are but simple, yet wretched farmers, not a grain to their name.

They appeal to all to be happy with the possessions stolen from them,
And not demand more, to "retrieve stolen goods", for more would be their life.
Forgive them for their scandalous appeal, *kotwal,* I assure you they know their place.
They know who they are, they are but humble farmers;
kotwal, leave this subject unworthy of your concern.

The beggars arrive before the hospices open; they seem to ask as soon as they spot an open palm, they wag their tails as soon as they spot a crumb, salivate as soon as they sense a drop of blood. They cry like crocodiles, smile like hyenas. What I would give to wipe their greedy smiles from their small faces and emaciated thoughts, what I would give to see the wretched vanquished, to see these rulers, dictators, taxmen, vigilantes, and those who cover their jackets carved with human leather, with saintly garb. They beg for my hard-earned money, my allegiance, my faith, my ideology, my souls, or even try to snatch them. I shall fight them forever; I have nothing to give though my reserves are plenty.

I Have Nothing To Give

My spirit is not worth much, sirs, my say holds little value.
The nod and your absence of contradicting my humility is not helping your case.
I refuse to bargain with you for my ideological allegiance,
I'm not a traitor, I only disagree with you, and you seem to turn deaf now.

Of course, it's hard to hear over clutter, it's hard to hear over the shouts,
The screams of accusations of treachery, the appeals to gather clubs and sticks and resolve to lynch,
The pleading intelligentsia, the voice which dares to object,
For I refuse, or rather, have nothing to give to you, I have nothing to offer.

I received my wages (the notes stink of sweat) only yesterday, and the bell rings for me.
For a portion of the notes I hold, for a portion of my earned subsistence.
In return I receive empty promises of better roads, sweeter water, and the health of my compatriots,
Or threats to jail and torture, which are much less empty, but I only have alms to offer, sir.

Forgive me for holding on to what little I have,
My spirit, my resolve, my free thoughts, my
conscience, my money.
They may be plenty now, but a single unit is one too much
to offer you, and thus I am scarce.
I have nothing to give, I have but only alms to offer, sirs.

There are countless travesties of justice around the world, but by far the vilest form of injustice is to punish the victim outright. So many of our brethren as humans have been blamed for the slaps and punches and indignities they received, or rather, "invited". The heroes who sought justice for the wronged are portrayed as villains; these bastions of truth are viewed with suspicion instead of trust, they are stepped on instead of being put on a pedestal. We have had no qualms worshipping rocks and papers which represented our inner conscience and good, and rightly so. Yet, we have also had no qualms on trampling this morality, the sense of right and wrong, with our dirty, lowly feet, desecrating them to invisible powder. Let us hope to fix the broken, clean the dirt, of our morality. Let us reconsider, and try to remember, that we and they possess hearts and heartbeats, and be careful not to break them.

Heartbeat

Take heart, stranger, the bandit who stole your last drop of water will be found,
And punished, and extracted water from, the sweet elixir of justice,
Shall flow to you, engulf you, embrace you in an apology.
Think fast! Here go your clothes and figs and dates and children,
And so must you, unwanted heathen!

Take heart, scantily clad innocent, your dignity would be returned.
To the one foolish enough to grant you any, you thief, you wretched swine.
You swim in immorality; you stink of all things lowly.
You deserved more than the merciful lashes you have received.
And so, you shall be haunted in your homes, in your soulless life, death, and all you find comfort in.

You, who have been pushed by one of our own, have stumbled into the idol we worship.
It is you who have disturbed the peace of our land, and destroyed the infinite goodness in us.
And so must you be lynched and torn and desecrated and hunted, like the rat you are,

And so must all who resemble you and choose to harbor germs like you in their hearth,
We seek to exterminate, to reclaim our goodness.

We shall traverse through feces and stink of hate, and harbor fleas and moths of the wretched,
To regain our purity. We shall spill blood on our tunic to get rid of dirt like you.
We shall make sure your puny heart and all those it longs for exist no more,
Neither shall your wretched heartbeat, the first a crime against you, the second- a punishment for daring to seek justice.

Shame is a double-edged sword, it is rewarding to all when it is deserved, while its imposition, when undeserved, is a shame to society itself. But shame strips us of our material, our illusions with ourselves, and laying us bare of our jewels and fake lighting to imitate aura, and exposing our human underneath.

Stripped

You have put me through trials, and I am laid bare;
The rocks I swore lay beneath my tunic are but a lie, for the flab droops in shame.
Yet so have you shown yourself, your true self, your unattainable self
I apologize, for I was misled to feel I desire you, I want you, I deserve you.

You have shown my inflated hubris, and burst them with a tiny pin.
Such is your glory compared to mine, such is your strength against mine.
The nectar I was promised at the peak of this mountain is not for me to consume.
And thus, a life was not for me to deserve, a sacrifice was not for me to make.

I have let you down, and so have I been too, for a subject I thought was for me to pursue,
Was not for me to master. I am not jeered at for no one sees how bare I am within my clothes.
Yet the whips of sorrow, of treachery of my own thoughts compel me to screech,
Yet the taunts, the attempts of my own soul to talk and touch me make me uncomfortable.

Every Kafkaesque, surreally horrible moment and most ecstatic moments have usually been shown as parts of dreams one wakes up from, relieved or disappointed, in literature, film and our own simulated worlds. Extremes do exist in reality, yet the norm is to confine them to dreams. In this poem, I try to deplore such imprisonment, and explore if all those, almost psychedelic moments, were not mere dreams.

Dream

Pins on a beating heart while entrails are pulled out,
Anesthetics nowhere felt or visible, it's just the screams which tire one's own ears.
Each blink hurts, with a hope, with an obvious expectation for this nightmare to go away,
But it stays! But it still hurts, still stings, from the betrayal by reality.

A shopping spree with no limit on the card, and no lectures on consumerism?
Peace of mind, peace in society and peace in every battlefield?
A relieved back free of burdens weighing on the conscience?
A sigh and a mirthless expectation to snap out, yet the dream persists!

It still soothes! It still brings a smile, a sweet sacrifice
by reality.
I have explored both the poles, and felt them in their truth.
I have the privilege to exclaims, it's not always a dream.
I also say with caution, though to less surprise, a nightmare is not always false.

Something dangles by a weak, but enduring link, not leaving without a brave last stand. Is it hope? Is it burden? Is it the link with a soon-to-be estranged family member? Let's take a look at this dangling link.

The Parting Tooth

It is dangling, it will leave, and it shakes the foundations of the mouth.
The gums scream and protest and writhe in pain, at its unwelcome departure.
The ligament, holding strong since the start of my existence, is giving away.
I can't bear the gap, I can't bear the pain, my seeking, begging tongue only makes it hurt more.

There is a crunch only I can hear, beyond the consolations, the trivializing, the promises of a relieved life.
The stings when the coffee enveloped us was harsh, but the crunches we felt were worth it.
Together through chocolate and nutcrackers and walnuts and soups, together through pain and comfort.
The link dangles, the link weakens, and breaks off, like the crack of a whip.

The pain is easier to bear than the numb empty, the painful swimming in a pool of brine,
Is easier to bear than the water which rushes past the empty that used to be occupied,
Taunting in its wake, the inevitability of absence, of parting, of weakening links,
Why must we part? Why aren't we allowed to be in pain?
Why are we denied the painlessly painful tenant?

I had heard the keys jangling, yet they are nowhere
to be seen.
The sweat starts to trickle, as I miss that jangle, but hear
instead impending doom.
Why must the toy van lose itself on its nostalgic ride?
Why must a marble bounce and not leap back into the
pocket of our childhood?

Where did it go, the meaningless cluster of atoms which
made me and my past?
Why must I be deemed unworthy of not receiving peace,
and a little piece of what has gone by?
Why must I make do with secret voices and fleeting images
I can't share or retrieve,
Why must I make do with wide eyes waiting for a
reprimand the next day, for my negligent sin?

The glory? Lost. The treasure? Lost. The heads held high
and first places? Lost.
A thousand street lamps left behind, and I now miss the light.
I have lost my senses, my pride, my desire to even search,
there remained only misery.
A miserable, stationary, pointless yell, forgetting squalor,
yelling, "Where did it go?"

BLAH
BLAH
BLAH
BLAH
BLAH
BLAH
BLAH
BLAH
BLAH
BLAH
BLAH
BLAH
BLAH
BLAH

Terrible scenes of old age, illness, death and destruction influenced a prince to abandon his worldly life and be nothing less than a selfless saint with his own philosophy of detachment from material joys, establishing a religion for millennia to persist, and is still followed by millions. However, these vices of the world still exist, yet rarely do we have the same urge to achieve immaterial fulfilment and "Nirvana" and "Enlightenment". Even when these pains of the world are not hidden for selfish purposes of whitewashing one's territory, they are rendered invisible, either to us or by us. In our frenzy of hopping from one mall to the other, one monument to the other, one party to the other, these scenes are barely even registered from the corners of our eye, blurry, warped.

Warp

It's magical, the lights, the crowd, the booming speakers,
The frenzied kids, the hide and seekers,
The tight grip on our hands leading to places yet to see,
The overwhelming of the five senses, the annoying tugging of my tee.

The rush of a stampede hides the malnourished mother with her sickly child,
The boom of my favourite song deafens me to the wails of the street dweller, legs crushed,
The appeals for alms, the pained shrieks, in comparison to the drums and yells of joy, seem mild.
Those scenes are warped, those screams, those begs are hushed.

Scan the crowd for your lost company, but ignore the humans without dignity,
Turn your eyes, avert your eyes from the inevitable of the world.
They are everywhere, the ghosts, the zombies screaming for my help.
Yet they are blurry, they are muted, they are faint, they are warped.

One moment we revel in company and swim in a joyous ocean of giggles, while an invisible, sharp jolt changes all that. Each chuckle stings, each giggle attacks like a taunt, and the pure, joyous frenzy is struck. We are shot, and we want to crawl back to the infirmaries of our lonesome.

Bullets

The shrapnels fly and land on the skin, attracted like a magnet,
A magnet inviting the scorns, the unease, ridding of the peace of mind,
A magnet serving justice and pain to the one which deserves a dose of sorrow,
To curb one's outburst of frenzied, uncivilized joy, unseemly and seditious.

The company and the ecstatic giggles now seem like monsters, suffocation.
The humor we yell joyfully now seem like daggers, to crucify one's conscience.
The bullets have come with a vengeance, to avenge the denial of their existence.
To break the blissful, temporary illusion of peace and satisfaction, for the sake of some cruel balance.

The bullets have come, with a vengeance, to make one squeal in pain,
And open one's eyes to the work to which one was blind.
The bullets have come to complete God's work, God's cruel, cruel work.
The bullets have come. You were part of a tribe, and the jeers it threw at the isolated.
Now you are the lone part of the tribe, bullet stricken, jeered by the tribe of the isolated.

There are some mere objects whose loss (as in the spatial, literal sense of the word) would correspond to a loss in our own peace of mind. An expensive but lost calculator is all the more dear if someone else paid for it. An object lost in the swamp is all the more dear if someone else must search for it. The burden of knowing that someone else must bear the burden you deserve is a burden nonetheless. Anything lost is all the more dear if there is collateral damage.

Collateral Damage

When I lean in for an embrace, I only receive the deceiving,
empty wind.
When I search for a penny, I only grasp a
horrifying nothing.
They say darkness is the root of our fears, but a dark room
is a fairy tale.
A dark, empty pocket, or a closet however, shall perpetually
haunt our callous souls.

Company only makes the empty worse, for this company is
your debtor.
I'm indebted to this company, who shall search the lost for
me, or search for it's own property.
I shall rather be the victim than the perpetrator, I shall
rather share the burden,
Than be it, than cause it, than know it. I shall throw
rather than receive the accusing glance, something I know
I deserve.

I'm in debt, and the collateral is my inner peace,
The sense of innocence and a guilt free life extorted by the
situation.
There has been damage dealt, travesties committed, and I'm
the criminal.
I must be put to trial in front of all the collateral damage.

This is a prayer to let the world conform to my ideals, my principles, and what I think is universally right, and also an appeal to grant me the sense and strength to accept my double standards and hypocrisy.

Let There Be

Let sense prevail, let the definition of humanity not be corrupted,
It's dignity not be violated anymore; its sanctity be respected.
Let us recognize that innocent lives who deserve compassion exist as well, let us be liberated from the veil of constant suspicion,
A veil we wove ourselves, the smog of cheating and scamming and stepping on fellow beings which feel pain too without batting an eye, we emitted ourselves.

Let there be no double-faced malice with contradictory views,
Let there be no prying eyes of malice, but only gaze of appreciation on the right things.
Let "me time" and "we time" be both cherished, let innocent familial or friendly mingling be considered right, instead of vain and ulterior.
Let there be no doubt, let there be trust, let there be actions and intentions warranting that trust.

Let there be no hecklers in an auditorium of expression and justice.
Let there be no oppressive, deafening silence when such an auditorium and all it represents be ransacked and ruined.
Let there be no silent hecklers who only wish for the defeat and downfall of the others.
Let there be strength, granted to me, to concede the difference between what I keep preaching and droning about, and what I do and am still inclined to do.

Short Stories

Judas is the Hero

"Swine!"

Ashish screamed at Tej. They were in a sweet, big old mansion on a leafy, posh suburb of Delhi.

Family reunions turning into good-old fashioned brawls over misunderstanding of banter, taunt duels, a murder or two, slighting of kith and kin over minor etiquettes. I sure would miss them.

I am Prince, the "heir" to this dungeon. But I am not going to fight over the ownership of a curse. My father, and my late mother, made this mansion to house the unemployed yet egoistic wing of our "family". In other words, pretty much the whole of it. Today, cancer fetched both of them and the family

The reason I don't want to go after it is that it would break all my ties with the people who I consider my real family. My son and my wife. They do not want me to follow the path of greed, knowing it would create rifts, and one thing we all know about rifts is that one moment, you are not living so cautiously and relax a bit, and the next moment, You. Fall. Down.

I am not a big fan of that.

Now back to the duel. This is between Ashish and Tej, the two "leaders" (although they show the qualities of slimy parasites instead of leaders) of the families of the two makers of the Mansion. Not that they have run out of taunts and money for suing each other at court, because they didn't and never will, for they have sucked both my parents' net value and blood. By now, it shouldn't be surprising that only a resource with economic value has kept the two branches of the family together. It was not endowed to either on the will. Now they challenged each other to a duel, as if all the years of taunt duel weren't enough. But this is much less toxic. All feelings, even though all malicious, were clear. All expressions, all the dialogues, were, for the first time meant in this meaningless "family".

I, the very man devoid of all feelings towards all the actions carried out by these two clans, was, for once, surprised. Ashish threw the first punch, and before you knew it, it was daggers and blood all over, and we didn't even collect daggers, which is surprising, given how fittingly we fit the role of a murderous, slimy colony of a dysfunctional family.

I beamed!

I never smile, let alone beam at a family event.

Both were known for their rage. In fact, even the two sections of the family who are spiteful of each other tried to stop them.

But they wouldn't ever trade anything in this world for a good brawl against their enemies.

It was a massacre. By next morning, the children of both the families were orphaned.

I called the police, me being the only adult who survived, being aloof from all events involving the clans. The police questioned me, I got released unscathed. A bit of soap in eyes convinces everybody, doesn't it?

I went back home. My wife hugged me and cried profusely.

She asked, "Are you okay? Do you need to go to the hospital?"

She then saw my unscathed body and the smile on my face, and then froze.

I beamed, again.

The very thing that caused my spiteful family's death was in my hand.

"Mission accomplished!"

Debt

Louis was a free man. He was behind those bars that he dreaded so much for ten years. The reason was counterfeiting, fraud, money laundering and straight-out stealing. Before being caught, he brought to the streets twenty families and shut down ten businesses through unlawful means. By the time the officials arrested him, a third of Besancon was bankrupt and only his businesses were there, giving him complete monopoly over the city.

Now, he was in debt. He owed at least 3.4 million euros to 35000 people. His businesses were shut down, and he was slighted. He was denied a job anywhere because of his tremendous debt and reputation. Things never looked more dire.

His only chance was to become an entrepreneur.

He didn't have much talent except hustling. But, he did have a talent in experimenting and innovating food.

So he thought, why not invent a new type of, maybe, mustard, the pride of nearby Dijon?

Of course, he would have a lot of completion. But, then again, he didn't have anything to lose, literally. So he gave it a go.

Unfortunately, his supplies were low, very low. All he had was some grapes, carrots, wine, and apple cider vinegar in meagre quantities. He didn't even have mustard, the main ingredient.

So, he turned to his past passion: - stealing.

He stole the mustard posing as a peasant from one of the lush fields of Burgundy.

He already had a cauldron, thankfully. Now all he needed to do is start experimenting.

Mustard with grapes? Absolutely not! Preposterous!

Mustard with garlic? Disastrous!

Mustard with apple cider vinegar? Fine, but not very original.

Mustard with garlic, apple cider vinegar and wine? That did taste good, and it was original!

Of course, he did not get the perfect "Besancon mustard" so easily. He overcame different hardships. Hooligans whom he owed money to, protesters, and former businessmen whom he stripped off of their wealth were constantly threatening to destroy his now poorly house and even received death threats. When he informed the spiteful police and asked for protection, they simply laughed it off and he was even hurt by a panhandler whom he supposedly owned money to. To add insult to the injury, he even recognized him, his best friend Claude, whom he was partners with before cheating him, fetching all his money and forcing their whole family to beg for basic needs such as food.

But now, his recipe for the perfect "Besancon mustard" was finished! All he needed was a survey from the people, and, since most of Besancon wanted his harm, he went to nearby cities and towns for the taste test, by walking, so was his determination and desperation.

All he had in his pocket was ten euros, for his food, which too, unfortunately, was stolen by a group of juveniles. Now all he had was his precious mustard. From Belfort to Langres, Vesoul, Dole, and finally, the very birthplace of the mustard itself, Dijon. He realized he was being too ambitious and did not expect a good reply, but he was surprised and not disappointed. His Dijon's people loved his samples.

This sensation, this sense of achievement was not felt by him even during his heists! This excitement, this racing of heart was very new to him. For the first time did he feel this tingling in his nerves! He decided, tomorrow, he will patent the mustard.

As a he lay in a lodge in Dijon whose sympathetic owner made him stay, Louis lay down in a comfortable, soft bed for the first time, his mind flooding with emotions, chief of whom were regret and the death threats and attacks on him by people whom he owed money to.

The only one who wasn't so vengeful yet had all the reasons to be was a former illegal child employee, who lost his poor family when they were killed in an occupational hazard in a cloth factory, leaving him with no money, when he went to work for Louise. Like every one of his former employees, he too was cheated of his wage, only that his condition was much more dire than any of them.

He then thought, "But, let bygones be bygones, and anyway, once I get the patent, I will repay each of them"

Tomorrow, Paris it is.

Louise retched and retched his belly out. He gave up all hope in life. He rushed upstairs the patent building, without hesitating, falling to end his pitiful, regretful, unwanted, miserable presence.

All of this madness, this drastic decision, was forced by the event two minutes ago.

He rushed inside the building, gave the patent officer a sample of the mustard. His veins threatened to burst, his heart was beating much faster than usual, he became aware of the slightest of sounds in the building.

The first of the two phases which led to the lethal decision had arrived.

The patent officer said, "Mr. Louise, the same mustard was patented yesterday by a very enterprising and talented young man."

Louise's shock was too much to be handled by him, hyperventilating, wondering who it was.

Then, he saw one of the juveniles who stole his ten euros, appear. Louise, although weak, did not hesitate to strangle him.

The boy gently released himself from the weak grip, laughed, and told him, "Oh, you poor man! Cheating countless people, acquiring so much wealth, yet look at your pitiful condition! I was just a little orphan then and a juvenile delinquent now, yet I have enough money to buy myself a small flat and go to college! Thankfully, unlike you, I chose your poorly jar of mustard instead of your famished purse!"

Jacket

As his mind was racing, with thoughts not really malignant, thoughts like, would he rather finish up an easy job nice and tight, leaving no loose ends, or go halfway through a difficult one, with both having the same level of job done, both leaving the same to be left to be done. As his face was frozen, wondering, blissfully oblivious to his surroundings, he left all to be wondered, with his muscles taking over the crucial job of hoisting himself down the steps of the bus, and carrying him back to his house, as he, but only, wondered.

His muscles continued on his daily procedure of gutting out his school bag after a tiresome, and oftentimes, infuriating day, a day at a place he often loathed for suppressing his blissful world of thoughts, with rude interruptions in the form of friends (the ones left, anyway) beckoning for him to play, and call to duty, to write so many, many words, all of which, he thought, mere wastage of ink. Out went those books, those notebooks, those tiffin boxes, the bottle? Phew....here it was.

Where's the jacket?

That jacket worth 600 bucks and absence of virtue-filled, annoying naggings about wastage, inattentiveness, and the value of money, looks grey with white spots, where is it? He seemed to be probing with his eyes. It was just a jacket, something he could afford to buy from his own pocket money and be left plenty with. He was grown up too, a moody teenager, and seemed to tolerate less and less rebukes. You know, the way teenagers are, and his parents aligned themselves to his way eventually, he tried to convince himself. Yet, he wondered if his free trial of escaping without consequences was over, if his admittedly spoiling parents reached their breaking point. He resolved to wait till Wednesday to inform them of the unfortunate case of the missing jacket, when he could buy the jacket from the school's apparel store.

So two days.

48 hours' worth of moral luggage. Surely that's not too rough? 48 hours to ponder why he was at a point in time when he could easily keep mum about staying up late, not following orders, and bunking, when confronted, yet getting trampled from pressure about keeping shut, not even lying about the lost jacket as his parents were due to arrive from there on Sunday. 48 hours of regret, of guilt, of debts of gratitude to the parents, deserved feelings, he didn't feel in a long time. 48 hours of regret for this prudential saver of money, this fiscally conscious teen to contemplate the scandalous fact that he pays 1200 to own one single jacket worth 600. And he closes his eyes.

Tuesday, 6.15 A.M, right before his school bus comes to pick him up: He calls his parents and cracks, to his own surprise. The jacket was in a hanger on his cupboard, hauntingly present, hanging, taunting, demanding an apology, staring intensely. If fear at FINDING the jacket, finding the lost was punishment, so be it.

Fortune

Rishi was bankrupt. He haggled with every money lender, most of them shady and sly. One, Damodar Ray, worked as an accountant for the Indian Railway Company under the British. Safe to say, his slyness was not unexpected, given that he was working under the foxes himself.

Rishi's brother, Mani (gem in Bengali) was anything but a gem. Every day, he wasted away, indulging himself in alcohol. He was of working age. In fact, job offers offering him enough salary to support his vast family and enough surplus to lead a luxurious life came at his door, thanks to his late father's high reputation, rank and nepotism. Rishi, however, was not as lucky as he was not exactly a favourite of the family, even though he being the sole breadwinner. He was not educated and alas, was not a spoilt wastrel like his brother.

The reason was that he had a dark complexion. To no surprise, he was literally treated like a slave by his mother, who was dependent on him. Yet, it was much different from his brother. He was treated like a king, and the same brother who tortured Rishi was dependent upon him for his very well-being and survival.

Rishi was, naturally fed up, and totally wanted to abandon them. He was not even given a square meal some days, while Mani became fat at the very expense of Rishi. They went as far as to attacking him when he went to fetch water in his own house. He had to drink from a nearby pond.

One day, Rishi was searching for another job as labourer, when he became thirsty and went to the pond. He saw a flyer, reading:-

For coloured men

"Job at Uganda! Stable job as labourer at Mombasa! Work for the Uganda Railway Company for the British!"

"Handsome salary!"

For interview, report to the Writer's Building, Calcutta

He felt his pulse grow! He felt his heart beat faster! He felt his heart thudding at his ribs, he was going to be free from this suffocating environment of his hometown! He was going to be free! Free from his diabolic mother, who was his mother only by name! Free from his wastrel brother, spoilt to the core, not understanding his value! Free from this sleepy town of narrow-minded zombies!

He marched to Calcutta, his only beacon of hope!

Rishi's lean, muscular body was the only thing that made him pass the physical test, his gateway to freedom! He decided in his mind, that enough with principles and values, enough of cowering and groveling, enough of meagre sums of money for tremendous work! He was not going to send any remittance back home for his ungrateful mother and that sorry excuse for a brother. Let his mother cry for his spoilt son, as he drinks and wastes him to death!

It was 2 years since Rishi came back to India. He now struck a fortune in Mombasa. Although subject to racial profiling, the British officials went easy on him compared to his African colleagues, who were given much less salary and had to do much more work. In fact, his best friend had died from exhaustion and not even a single penny was offered to his family as compensation. In fact, his family went as far as to sell his son to slavery. When he heard of it, he decided to take them under their wing. Compared to them, his status was much, much better, he being lighter than his other colleagues, and he being an Indian, a citizen of the jewel of the British Empire! He had free lodging in a pretty bungalow, free healthcare, and he was also invited to parties! All of this was thanks to education which he secretly received from the O'Conrads, an American family who decided to make his life, along with many other African's lives better through education. This was the first time a coloured individual received a post as high in the Office of the Registrar of records of the Uganda Railway company. He was left with enough surplus to live a luxurious life in Calcutta.

But, unfortunately, he got the shock of his life!

He realized, from his slighted, coloured neighbour, that all the torture, all those years of humiliation, was unintended. His Brahmin village used to stone to death any coloured immediately after being born. To save him from his dreary fate, his father and mother had to keep him a secret, a closely guarded secret. To secure him a future, if not by being a learned man, he had to be kept hardened. He had to be emotionally and physically strong, which was required for the survival of the bleak life of a coloured. To keep him emotionally strong, his mother had to make his life miserable. Even though it was eating her from within. He didn't believe his neighbour's eye-opening tale.

He found it out the hard way.

His mother was in her deathbed, due to her attempt to end her life by swallowing poison, due to the guilt of her torturing her own son, even though it was responsible for his present state of aristocracy and even his very survival, as he had to be alerted all day to run or fight with mobs trying to end his life. His mother's last wish was to see, or at least know her son was safe.

As for his wastrel brother, Your Honour, I had to kill Rishi. Your Honour, I was bitter, because although not evident, my little brother was always favoured, albeit it looked quite the opposite. My mother had to act as if she favoured me to make him emotionally strong, from a very ripe age! She even used to forget my name nearly every day. This shaped me to be the wastrel, bitter, monster of an excuse for a son and a brother.

I failed as both.

Having said so, I plead guilty, Your Honour. I am ready to face the noose of my fate.

Yours faithfully,

Mani Charan Das.

Prisoner:-896

To Whom It May Concern

Ashish had come back to his village after his contract ended, empty-stomached, thin pocket and barefoot. You see, not a lot of labourers are lucky enough to get a substantial contract for work accompanied by a good salary. So his present conditions were understandable and nothing out of the ordinary. But what wasn't ordinary was his notebook. No living person had ever laid eyes upon the notebook, filled with images of agonized people, destruction, his strange addiction with spirits and his negligence towards me after that incident. You will get to hear it.

Now, I must introduce myself. I am Shakti, Ashish's friend. He used to work in the coal mine near Raniganj, West Bengal When his contract ended, he left the mine in a very fortunate moment, as the next day, the local paper was headlined:

"Miners in Raniganj coal mine dead, only survivor left before blast thanks to best friend's sacrifice, government under pressure from human rights activist over safety"

Ashish was relieved, yet at the same time, grieving his friends, and also for some reason, scared.

I dreamt, I was in the mine, then a sudden blast burned me into ashes. My soul, agonized, shocked was being pulled upwards by some force. The force comforted me, yet, at the same time, agonized me!

I shook myself awake. I went to Ashish's house. He was my best friend after all.

I knocked at his door. No answer. I knocked a little louder, hoping he was home.

I saw his peeping eyes, having a tired and for some reason, terrified look!

I heard him rushing inside his house, and dangerous retching sound!

"Ashish! Ashish! Are you okay?"

Still no answer.

I yelled to the people in the streets! What happened to Ashish?! My mind, a race of emotions, my heart, pumped with adrenaline, curiosity, under pressure! No one was even looking at me, let alone answer!

The next moments were a blur. I had no idea how, but I went inside his house and above a pool of vomit, I saw a cold, lifeless Ashish, hanging!

That's when my body gave in, or at least felt so! I still don't know how, but, I felt like retching, retching till my energy was sapped, retching till all of my organs which were vital, but now that my best friend, the friend who understood me best, ceased to exist, was pretty much pointless! But, again, I couldn't retch.

I tried to hang myself through the same noose which made him leave me.

Just when I tried to hold the noose, it just went through me, as if my body was made of clouds.

And that is when it hit me.

The town, the house, my friend's body.....all dissipated like the closing scene of an act.

I was in the clouds.

Don't blame me. I did tell "no **living** person had ever laid eyes upon the notebook", and blame yourself for your inattentiveness! Didn't you see the local's headline, "only survivor left before blast thanks to best friend's sacrifice".

Plastic Lid

With a limp in her legs, and her flexibility curved, she came to stay at her daugther's house. Not out of free will, but out of compulsion. She liked living alone in her condominium apartment, alone and free to do whatever she feels, behave however she wishes. She does like her family, but freedom, to her is worth more. Ironically, freedom for her is being stationary guilt-free, free from the watchful, critical gaze of her daughter and her family. She was a good daughter; she took care of all of her needs. Nourishment, medications, finance, every material necessity. Yet there was a lack of warmth between them, a coldness, ever since her father went away. Almost as if her imperfections were highlighted.

Though her husband did help her immensely and made her life convenient, he was vulnerable to urges of mocking the lady. He and the son poke fun of her lethargic and sometimes ludicrous manners, and tease her seeming self-pity. She, though was oblivious to all of it.

One day, when the daughter and son-in-law took out their laptops and expressed their desire to work in peace from the house, she approached his rather irate grandson, who did take care of her needs, filling bottles of water for her and doing all the household chores in the absence of his parents, while also completing homework. She wanted to chat with him, even though there had been friction between her and the difficult teenager, eager to spot any imperfection, any malpractice in her.

"What now Gramma?"

"That's no way to talk to an elder, especially a lady. I tell ya, you will have trouble finding one, in all of the city!"

"Oh right, you are right. My whole goal in life is to have a relationship status. Thanks Grams, that's exactly what I needed from you! I needed some advice about something I have no interest in, not some stupid namby-pamby HEARTWARMING love from you and stupid tender talks which I would have done quite well with!" "Oh lad, so this is what it's all about? She did ramble on about, "Atashi, you better behave well with your family, will do bloody well for you and them. What's the opposite of collateral damage, again?" Felt spectacular getting rid of that old bone, but maybe she was right?"

"Took you long enough to get the hint after her 'ramblings'. And you dare wonder why we are not so friendly?"

"Listen now dear-"

"Why don't you do so first? You shall get what you shall reap and all those other clichés, you better apply 'em on you."

"Well", with a cracked voice she croaked, "I guess that is that".

She walked away, at a pace so brisk Jamie began to suspect what was really wrong with her.

"Gramma, listen-"

"Wait, Gramma-"

But she didn't have a care in the world. With dry eyes, she slammed the door of her room...

And after gathering herself, after gathering her impatience, and anger, steadying her breath, she opened the door.

"Look Deb", she started, as Deb reared back, astonished by that wild, passionate, jarring look on those rather unassuming black eyes. "I have better things to do, better sensations to feel than be your nurse. I have a right to have a life, and a better quality than your parents at that. Enough of tolerating you burdens. And leave...me...ALONE."

A gaping Deb, stood frozen, and scurried back to his room as his cruel, burdening Gramma bellowed Shoo!

With a teacup in her hands, at spiritual peace, she rested herself on the metal railings as a shield from the great, empty height, ending to a hard, fatal, and very solid anticlimax.

As she savoured the last drops of that Earl Grey she had been having since time immemorial, she left the responsibility, the hidden cruelty of her parasitical corrupt offspring and co siphoning her and her late beloved's belongings, the sheer audacity of her grandson in a self-made delusion of lack of love received from her, the blissful memories when she raised her children well, with her husband, the burden of all these fiery tangled chains, Deb locked in his room, stove put on, which just like her own cruel, barely human soul, set free from a sinful house, which, in her opinion, failed to become a home. As she steadies her frail self on the railing, she fell off, just like from a metal, opaque glass, a plastic lid.

Demon of The past

It has been 2 whole days since Bertram was stranded in Baffin Island. An unprecedented blizzard ruined all his plans of scaling Canada's northern tundra. The Inuits tried to provide supplies the first day, but the next day, the blizzard was raging and it was impossible to communicate with anyone or travel anywhere. He rationed whatever supplies he got from the Inuits the day before. The sleet was stinging his face, and the wind froze his ears. His whole body felt stiff and numb from the cold of the place.

He recalled a local Inuit legend about a demon called Mahahaa. It was known to kill people just by tickling them. The legend goes like this:

"Once there was a couple who lived all alone. They had no children so the woman had to stay all alone every time the man went to hunt. While the woman was alone she happened to go into the porch and had a dreadful encounter with a Mahahaa. The thing tickled her to death, so she lay dead in the porch still smiling away. The husband was furious to discover his wife dead in the porch. From the look in her face he knew she was tickled to death. Still furious he waited in his iglu. When night came he went to bed with his clothes on leaving the entrance wide open. Suddenly he heard someone coming in laughing away as hard as it could. As it laughed, it said, "Oh my dear father in law, ha, ha, ha, ha, haa." Sure enough the thing attacked the man. It climbed up on the bed platform and started to tickle the man. He grabbed the thing by the ankles and swung it on the floor. Now in the old days as the iglu got old, the floor becomes icy. As he was bashing the thing on the ice floor, it just kept on laughing away as hard as ever. It did not even appear to feel any pain what so ever. Thinking he could not kill it he enticed it to with him to the water hole. At the water hole he asked it to take a drink. As it bent to take a drink he pushed it to the hole and drove it under the ice with an ice scoop. Finally the thing died."

He heard of this legend at story time in school every Friday. His mind wandered off to old memories of the quaint suburb where he lived, the memories of him cycling the neighbourhood, of him basking in the suburb the few times in summer when the neighbourhood became sunny, of gossiping with friends.

Suddenly, a shiver went down his spine. His nerve became to tingle, and a mix of frustration, anxiety and sadness! A kind of anguish flowed through his blood, that caused him to convulse.

He heard a shrill, eerie laugh-like whizz coming from the wind which transformed into a laugh. He tried to locate where it came from and saw a silhouette of a long, monkey-like humanoid with really long fingers. Bertram was too disoriented to form intelligible sentences so he kept mumbling and yelling at it.

But he was in his senses enough to realize it was the Mahahaa!

He started feeling a tingling all over his body which morphed into full on tickling. He was laughing hard; he began to shake and gave his last guffaw!

"BERTY, STAY! STAY! CALM! BE CALM!", the nurses exclaimed as they tried to control a hyperactive, chuckling Bertram.

"Mrs Ostrend, can you please tell me what happened with Bertram over here?"

A crying Mrs. Ostrend told the doctor, "Bertam was six when he was betrayed by his family and friends, the same people who made him they loved him, the same people who made him laugh."

The cold of betrayal.

The sleet of truth which stings him.

The endless snow of regret and memory.

People who can make you laugh from the outside can make you cry and kill you from the inside.

The Folly of the Notes

Maddox was frustrated. And that would be an understatement, for a run-of-the-mill person would be just frustrated after repeated attempts to sing or play a musical instrument in tone. Maddox, however, was not a mere run-of-the-mill musician. He was one of those artistic people, who, it is more or less accurate to say, lived a life of penance, refusing vast sums of money offered in reverence by awestruck, very wealthy men and women. He was under the impression that no amount of money could be worth his performance, no amount of worship could do justice to this god of music. Call him proud and overconfident, heck, some people even called him a village idiot to have such excess pride in his work. Go ahead, try! But all those who went to witness him, snickering, returned and had the same reaction: a sudden urge to donate, no, fulfil their debt (in their reformed opinion) to this master of music by giving all their possessions to him. But I do have to, albeit grudgingly, agree that Maddox was a perfectionist, and also grudgingly agree that his performance was worth every single shred of his extreme pride.

But today, in the Bolshoy, where he dreamed to perform, Maddox was going through hell. He had a bad case of not being able to vocalize and tune himself. His fingers hovered over the keys of the grand piano, but it seemed to resist. His fingers struggled to disobey their master and play the wrong tune. All of it sounded so imperfect, so unrelated, so alien, so.......wrong, that he cried in anguish. His pale face was red from anger and frustration, his nerves felt frayed, his hands, full of adrenaline, were rushing and were shaking! He got very angry when some butlers in striped fluorescent green and white shirt and striped black and white hats took hold of him and escorted him out of the vast, royal opera. The butlers were not worthy of touching The Master of Audio! They threw Maddox into a car with blue flashing lights, probably to signal the arrival of the great musician, maybe to calm him and take him to a hotel, to treat the Emperor of Tunes in the way he deserved. He felt very empty and obligated to enchant the crowd, and their insistence to give all their possessions to me, usually food products like eggs, tomatoes and flour, and occasionally accessories like shoes. But so far, it just felt very strange and otherworldly, because I know Russian and overheard the conversation between two of the butlers.

"Who is this madman? Is he a saboteur?"

"Let me check his records." The lady butler took out a long, thick book. The lady muttered "Maddox Gustavich, has narcissistic personality disorder, no criminal records, talks with himself in third person"

"So just a harmless little madman."

www.ingramcontent.com/pod-product-compliance
Lightning Source LLC
La Vergne TN
LVHW041206150826
845673LV00001B/302

* 9 7 9 8 8 9 2 3 3 5 8 7 4 *